RESTLESS HEARTS

Studies for Young Adults

Where Do I Go Now, God?

leader guide

Alex Joyner

ABINGDON PRESS / Nashville

RESTLESS HEARTS
WHERE DO I GO NOW, GOD?
Leader Guide

Copyright © 2007 by Abingdon Press

All rights reserved.

Scripture quotations in this publication, unless otherwise indicated, are from the *New Revised Standard Version of the Bible,* copyrighted © 1989 by the Division of Christian Education of the National Council of the Churches of Christ in the United States of America, and are used by permission.

Scripture quotations marked (NLT) are taken from the *Holy Bible,* New Living Translation, copyright © 1996. Used by permission of Tyndale House Publishers, Inc., Wheaton, Illinois 60189. All rights reserved.

This book is printed on acid-free, elemental chlorine-free paper.

ISBN 978-0-687-33556-5

07 08 09 10 11 12 13 14 15 16—10 9 8 7 6 5 4 3 2 1
MANUFACTURED IN THE UNITED STATES OF AMERICA

CONTENTS

SESSION PLANS

PREFACE

I am a very unlikely person to write a curriculum on vocation. I was propelled into ordained ministry by a story written by Annie Dillard that was read aloud by a clergy mentor. In a short meditation entitled "Living Like Weasels," Dillard offered me an image of a creature so tenacious that it would seek out the point of life of its prey and attack it from sheer instinct, withholding nothing.[1] Listening to that story as a recently-graduated college student working as a radio news director, I knew that I had not yet discovered my point of life. Within the year, I was in seminary.

But twenty years later I would still be hard-pressed to say what my point of life is. Far from being the ending of my vocational journey, my encounter with the weasel was only the beginning. I have followed a calling that led to cross-cultural appointments in Texas and England, rural local church ministry, further education, writing, and campus ministry. Along the way I have discovered that I am not alone in thinking of vocation as an open question and not a destination. Perhaps that is why I am so attracted to the questions that motivate this study.

Restless Hearts grew out of a small group that began meeting during my time as the director of the Wesley Foundation at the University of Virginia. Drawing inspiration from Augustine of Hippo's famous confession that "our heart is restless until it rests in [God],"[2] the small group allowed me to concentrate some of my thoughts on what vocation involves and to explore what was actually going on in the lives of college students, for whom the issue of vocation is a central concern. I will always be grateful for those late nights in the Willson game room of the Wesley Foundation when the Spirit inhabited the ordinary space of our common lives. Though I am sure to leave some of the principals of that group out, no listing of students I would want to thank could exclude Andrew Marshall, Joel Winstead, Matt Zimmerman, Virginia Leavell, and David Vaughan.

My other collaborators along the way include my fabulous colleague during many of my years in campus ministry, Deborah Lewis. Her challenge, encouragement, insight, and sharing of her own vocational wanderings all contributed greatly to this project emerging at all. Her life is a great testimony to C. S. Lewis' observation that sometimes "the longest way round is the shortest way home."[3] For all that she collects and shares along the way, I am grateful.

The most enriching thing about campus ministry is the steady stream of students passing through the doors, staying with us for a time, sharing their growth, their struggles, and their joys, and moving on to new adventures. So many of them bolster this work that I hesitate to name just a few; but certainly Jessie Smith, Brantley Craig, Meredith McNabb, Brian Johns, Laura Martin, Sara Porter Keeling, Sasha Miller, Sarah Willson Craig, Drew Willson, and Debbie Noonan cannot go unmentioned.

There were just as many hands urging me along to complete this process. My own family, Suzanne, Joel, and Rachel, endured many writing sessions that took me away from doing really important work, like watching reruns of *Lost in Space*. They are all a gift and a blessing to me. Colleagues, like Rhonda and Don Van Dyke Colby, Tammy Estep, and my covenant group on the Eastern Shore, have helped hold me to the writing task. Hogan Pesaniello has pushed me to deeper insights and valuing of the sometimes murky depths of my soul, something that has often emerged in the writing of this study. And what can I say about Jim Fossett, who so graciously adopted me as a writing partner and surrendered his office so that this could be finished? He even gave me fossils! Thank you.

To Pam Dilmore, who has been my long-suffering editor; Dow Chamberlain, who gave me the opportunity to write; and the whole staff of *FaithLink*, where my public writing began—I offer gratefulness and praise.

The journey is before us. Let's begin!

—*Alex Joyner*

---

[1] "Living Like Weasels," in *Teaching a Stone to Talk*, by Annie Dillard (Harper Perennial, 1988).
[2] *The Confessions of Saint Augustine*, translated by John K. Ryan (Doubleday, 1960); page 43.
[3] *Mere Christianity*, by C. S. Lewis (HarperSanFrancisco, 2001); page XIX.

INTRODUCTION

RESTLESS HEARTS
WHERE DO I GO NOW, GOD?

Welcome to Restless Hearts, a small-group study for young adults that will help them reflect upon who they are, upon what they want to do with their lives, and upon God's presence and care in the midst of their vocational journey. The young adults who participate in this vocational reflection study will:

- gain a sense of God's care for them
- understand more about their own personalities, identities, and gifts
- discover that a relationship with God is the primary vocation of all people
- view their life work and education or training as necessary for that work in light of God's purposes

- develop spiritual disciplines of prayer, Bible study, and personal reflection
- discover the value of and insights gained by participating with others in a small-group setting
- experience the freedom to explore some of their deepest questions and concerns regarding vocation and faith during this particular stage of their lives
- discover ways to help others as they search for purpose and meaning in their lives

CORE VALUES

The small-group study is grounded in the following values, which are reviewed in each of the six sessions:

- We are created to be related to God and others.
- Our vocation is more than our job.
- Baptism is the continuing reminder of who we are.
- Our careers should work in concert with our vocation, not against it.
- The key career question is not, "What do I want to do for the rest of my life?" but "Who am I, and what am I going to do next?"
- We discern our path by paying attention to the world around us and to what is happening within us.
- Spiritual disciplines help us discern God's calling.

"OUR HEART IS RESTLESS"

"For you have made us for yourself and our heart is restless until it rests in you."[1] The name of this study was prompted by these words of Augustine of Hippo (354–430), a North African bishop in the early church who found his vocation and sense of self through an examination of his life. Augustine's emphasis on self-reflection is most evident in his autobiographical work, *The Confessions of Saint Augustine.* Here, he begins with the affirmation that is central to the

Restless Hearts approach to vocational reflection—God has created us in such a way that we cannot fully understand ourselves apart from God; and since we often live our lives with an incomplete awareness of how we are related to God, we are discontented. Augustine encourages us to pay attention to the inner tuggings that pull us toward God, a condition he describes as having a restless heart.

At the same time that Augustine recognized how central his relationship to God was for him, he also knew that other relationships were important as well. In his *Confessions,* he walks back through his life retelling it in such a way that he sees the contributions that his mother, his teachers, and even children playing in a neighboring garden made to his vocational understanding. All of the parts of his life, even the parts he was not very proud of, were moments he could reclaim as times when God was present in the midst of relationships, drawing him toward a new vision of who he was.

One of Augustine's lasting legacies is his emphasis on self-reflection as a means to understanding God. The journey toward God is one that passes through the interior life of each person. This study follows the example of St. Augustine in looking at vocation through our identities as children of God through Jesus Christ. It is a Christian study that assumes that God is present in and calls all persons through their explorations of vocation. Who are we? Who did God create us to be? How does God want us to live? What are we to do with our lives? All the sessions invite young adults to consider these questions and others.

Session One, "Inside Out: Expectations," will help young adults identify the tensions that exist between their inner sense of values and calling and the expectations that others have for them. They will explore the benefits of listening for God both inside and outside of themselves as a part of the lifelong process of vocational discernment.

Session Two, "Passion and Vocation," helps young adults recognize that the passions that drive us are often unacknowledged and sometimes unappreciated. Uncovering what their passion—that is, what their hearts truly desire—is one way to listen for God and to explore vocation. This session invites them to listen to their passions as a way of listening for God.

Session Three, "Trusting the Gifts," helps young adults move to a deeper level of trusting that there is a purpose moving through their gifts. The session encourages them to claim their gifts and abilities as they identify their vocation.

Session Four, "Listening in the Shadows," helps young adults recognize that a vocational journey oriented toward God may lead them to despise or suppress those parts of themselves they feel are unworthy or unnecessary. However, there are treasures to be found when they search among their needs, anxieties, and places of brokenness for God's healing presence. They will be encouraged to explore the role that our "shadow side" plays in helping us listen for God.

Session Five, "Somebody's Calling Your Name," helps young adults discover that they can also claim their vocation as they meet God in the needs of the world. It encourages them to identify needs in the world around us that are crying out for response and to develop a pattern of engaging in acts of service and justice.

Session Six, "Taking Risks," helps young adults discover that risk is an invaluable tool for moving them from who they have been to who they are going to be. By consciously choosing to stretch themselves into areas where they know they will be required to change, they can experience greater trust in God and greater awareness of God's call. This final session provides the tools for identifying an action plan for their next steps in the vocational journey.

RESOURCE COMPONENTS

The resources and group sessions in this study function together to facilitate personal and group reflection about vocation, a key issue for most young adults. The resources include a workbook for each participant, a DVD for viewing during group sessions, and a leader guide.

Workbook

The workbook is designed for use by the group participants. Each person in the group should have his or her own copy. It contains stories, narratives, and information that invite reflection and response; and it will be used both during and outside of the session. The section entitled "Looking Ahead" will suggest an activity for participants' personal reflections in the time before you meet as a group again. The study invites participants to adopt the discipline of journaling through the course of these sessions. The workbook that each person receives not only offers resources for the sessions but also offers space for writing in between sessions. Not everyone is comfortable with writing. Years of frustration in school settings may make some group members reluctant to take on an exercise that involves traditional writing. Learning disabilities may compound that frustration. Therefore, responses in the workbook may take many forms: writing, drawing, use of symbols, or use of timelines. Some may even treat the workbook as a kind of scrapbook to collect pictures or items that are meaningful to them in response to the exercises. You should affirm all of these methods. What is most important is that participants use the workbook in order to reflect on the session topics, on the Scriptures, on the Core Values of the study, and on their lives.

DVD

The video segments on the DVD are designed to enrich and enhance the core content presented in each session. They are intended to inspire young adults to engage the questions that emerge from the topic of the session. These segments are 6–10 minutes long and will be viewed during the group sessions, as described in the leader guide. They are designed to facilitate group reflection and discussion in the sessions.

Leader Guide

The leader guide is designed to help you lead your group with confidence and inspiration. It contains all the information needed for leading your group. Detailed session plans give you easy-to-follow instructions, including what materials you will need and how to prepare the learning area. The plans also encourage you to set aside a time before the actual session to prepare yourself spiritually and to review your approach to the session.

SESSION FORMAT

As you will see in both the workbook and the leader guide, the sessions all have a similar format. Each week, you will lead your group through a sequence of activities that is described following this paragraph. This sequence of activities is designed to bring the group together; to create an environment for learning; and to help the group use videos, books, Scripture, and group discussion to explore vocation. Details of how to prepare for and implement these activities, week by week, are spelled out in the leader guide under "Session Plans" (pages 19–95). Each session includes the following sequence of activities:

Opening Worship: Each week when the group gathers, the session will begin with a worship experience. Restless Hearts *Where Do I Go Now, God?* uses stones and water to remind participants of baptism as a symbol of their identity as beloved members of God's family.

The Questions: This section offers stories and illustrations in the workbook and video segments that will invite young adults to engage the focus for each week's study through personal reflection and small-group discussion.

The Scriptures: Each session will explore specific biblical texts related to the session focus. The workbook contains a box entitled "Your Reflections on the Scriptures." Encourage the participants to respond to the questions in this box each week.

Your Life: Participants will reflect upon their lives and the Core Values that ground the study in a variety of activities included in this segment. The workbook contains a box entitled "Core Values and Your Life." Encourage participants to respond to the questions in this box each week.

Looking Ahead: This part of the session includes reading and journaling in the workbook. These activities will prepare participants for the next session. Encourage them to do these activities each week.

Closing Worship: Every session concludes with a worship experience related to the focus for the session.

HOW TO ORGANIZE A GROUP

In order to start a young adult study group, you may want to follow the steps below.

1. Read through the leader guide and the workbook. View all the video segments on the DVD. Think about the topic dealt with in the study, the issues it generates, and the Scriptures. Prepare to respond to questions that someone may ask about the study.

2. Develop a list of potential young adult participants. An ideal size for a small group is seven to 12 people. Your list should have about twice your target number (14 to 24 people). Encourage your local church to purchase a copy of the workbook for each of the young adults on your list. This is an invaluable outreach tool.

3. Decide on a location and time for your group.

4. Identify someone who is willing to go with you to visit the young adults on your list. Make it your goal to become acquainted with each person you visit. Tell them about Restless Hearts *Where Do I Go Now, God?* Give them a copy of the workbook. Even if they choose not to attend the group at this time, they will have an opportunity to study

the book on their own. Tell each person the initial meeting time, location, and how many weeks the group will meet. Invite them to become a part of the group. Thank them for their time.

5. Publicize the study through as many channels as are available through your local church, your campus ministry, and your community.

6. A few days before the sessions begin, give a friendly phone call or send an e-mail to thank all persons you visited for their consideration and interest. Remind them of the time and location of the first meeting.

HOW TO LEAD A GROUP

The role of the leader is to use the resources and facilitate the group sessions in order to help young adults reflect upon vocation. So what does a leader do?

A Leader Prepares

The leader guide contains specific instructions for planning and implementing the study. Generally speaking, however, a leader has some basic preparation responsibilities. These are:

Pray

Ask for God's guidance as you prepare to lead the session.

Read, View, and Reflect

Review the session materials and its Scriptures ahead of time. View the video segments. Jot down questions or insights that occur during the reading and during the viewing of the video segments.

Think About Group Participants

Who are they? What life issues or questions might they have about the theme? About the Scriptures?

Prepare the Learning Area

Gather any needed supplies, such as large sheets of paper, markers, paper and pencils, Bibles, audiovisual equipment, masking tape, Bible dictionaries and commentaries, and supplies needed for the worship experiences. If you are meeting in a classroom setting, arrange the chairs in a semicircle so that everyone can easily see the video segments that will be shown during the session. Make sure everyone will have a place to sit. Set up a worship center as described in the session plans.

Pray for the Group Participants

Before the participants arrive, pray for each one. Ask for God's blessing on your session. Offer thanks to God for the opportunity to lead the session.

A Leader Creates a Welcoming Atmosphere

Hospitality is a spiritual discipline. A leader helps to create an environment that makes others feel welcome and helps every participant experience the freedom to ask questions and to state opinions. Such an atmosphere is based upon mutual respect.

Greet Participants as They Arrive

Say aloud the name of each participant. If the class is meeting for the first time, use nametags.

Listen

As group discussion unfolds, affirm the comments and ideas of participants. Avoid the temptation to dominate conversation or "correct" the ideas of participants.

Affirm

Thank people for telling about what they think or feel. Acknowledge their contributions to discussion in positive ways, even if you disagree with their ideas.

A Leader Facilitates Discussion

Ask Questions

Use the questions suggested in the session plans or other questions that occur to you as you prepare for the session. Encourage others to ask questions.

Invite Silent Participants to Contribute Ideas

If someone in the group is quiet, you might say something like, "I'm interested in what you're thinking." If participants seem hesitant or shy, do not pressure them to speak. However, do communicate your interest.

Gently Redirect Discussion When Someone in the Group Dominates

You can do this in several ways. Remind the group as a whole that everyone's ideas are important. Invite them to respect one another and to allow others the opportunity to express their ideas. You may establish a group covenant that clarifies such mutual respect. Use structured methods such as going around the circle to allow everyone a chance to speak. Only as a last resort, speak to the person who dominates conversation after the group meeting.

---

[1] Ryan; page 43.

1

Session Plans

SESSION ONE
INSIDE OUT: EXPECTATIONS

Focus:

We live in the tension between our inner sense of values and calling and the expectations that others have for us. Listening for God both inside and outside of ourselves is the lifelong process of vocation.

Objectives:

- To explore interactions between internal and external tuggings related to our vocation
- To explore the values that motivate this study on vocational reflection

- To experience community and to grow in commitment to God, self, and one another during the study

Reflections for This Session

My father has a way of stretching the truth, and that's one of the things I love about him. I've known this ever since I was a child. On long car journeys to visit my grandparents in rural Tidewater Virginia, back in the days before handheld video games became a pacifier for bored children, my sisters and I could usually convince my father to tell us tales from when he was a child.

We never quite knew what we were going to get. Sometimes it would be a tale of his boyhood in the Depression. These were Tom Sawyer-like adventures such as sneaking under the flap of the tent that housed the cowboy films. I suspect those stories were mostly true. Other times he would tell dark and ominous tales about a headless dog that foreshadowed some great tragedy. Given the difficult realities of his early years when he lost a father and a brother to illness, I suspect there was some truth to those stories as well. At other times the sharing would be not so much a story as a collection of warm memories of the life he had known in the place to which we were headed.

The truth is that it was often hard to sort out fact from fantasy in these stories, but they all told a greater truth that made Tidewater Virginia a magical place for me. Through my father's stories I knew that life was adventurous, that there was tragedy and darkness along the way, but that somehow we have a place in this world and it is good. I have always been grateful for this early introduction to grace and for having a context in which to discover who I was.

This session is built around the belief that all of our lives are lived in the midst of converging stories. Some of those stories we write ourselves as we encounter others and the world. Other stories claim us before we have a chance to choose them. One way to explore this is by wading in the water.

Water is one of the essential symbols of the Christian faith. In the waters of baptism, God claims us and gives us a vocation as a child of God. Naming is an important part of the ritual of baptism, too, as we are each called by our unique name and joined to the name of Jesus Christ.

Many traditions in the Christian family baptize infants and young children. Parents, guardians, and other sponsors take on vows to raise the children being baptized with an awareness of God's love and intentions for their lives. The liturgy rehearses the story of God's grace and acts of salvation, and the community embraces the children as its own. Later, usually during adolescence, the children will be invited to take on the vows that have been made on their behalf and to take responsibility for living out God's good news as a part of the community. Other traditions in the Christian family practice believer's baptism. Persons are baptized in acknowledgement of God's grace, forgiveness, and new birth into the Christian family. In all cases, baptism signals one's identity as a beloved child of God.

Vocation is lived out in the creative tension represented by the sacrament of baptism. On the one hand, we arrive in the world as an absolutely unique individual, full of potential and promise that will be unfolded in ways that those around us cannot imagine. At the same time we do not arrive in isolation. We enter a context formed by the expectations of others and by narratives we didn't write. Before we are able to utter a word of preference, choices have already been made for us. Over time we are able to express more of our individual desires, but some things will always remain constant—our family history, our genetic make-up, and some of our general personality traits, for example.

Christians believe that one of those unchanging constants is God's outward-reaching love toward us. The waters of baptism are a sense reminder of the grace that goes before us, providing us with a secure starting place for all of our reflections on who we are and what we are meant to be.

Martin Luther, the great Protestant reformer of the sixteenth century, relied on his identity as a baptized Christian for daily strength and he encouraged others to say, "I am baptized" as an affirmation. In the face of conflict, anxiety, and uncertainty, Luther's baptism provided him with the clarity of vision that he needed.[1]

In this session we will wade into the water and begin a journey of vocational exploration together. We will listen to the stories that have been told to us and about us by others; and we will seek God's story in the inner movements of our souls.

Prepare for the Session

Let your preparation for the session be a time to pay attention to God and to the needs of group members as well as a time to review the content of the session. Find a quiet and comfortable place where you will not be interrupted. Have the DVD, a Bible, and the workbook available, in addition to the leader guide. Have paper and pen available to jot down notes, insights, and ideas. You may wish to keep these notes in a personal journal during this study.

Pray

Ask for God's guidance as you prepare for the session. Pray for the participants who will be a part of this session.

Read, View, and Reflect

As you read the leader guide, workbook, and Scriptures, and as you view the video segments, write down thoughts, insights, questions, and ideas that emerge for you. Also write questions that you think might emerge from the group.

Read the information about Restless Hearts *Where Do I Go Now, God?* in the introduction to the leader guide to make sure you understand the process for the sessions in the series. Anticipate questions group members might have about the study.

Review the Core Values described in the introduction (page 10).

Read the story of Hannah, Eli, and Samuel in 1 Samuel 1:9-18; 3:1-21. Read the story of Samson and his parents in Judges 13:1-7, 24; 14:1-20.

View the video segments for Session One, "Introduction" and "Inside Out: Expectations." If you have time, view all the video segments in the study in order to have a more complete overview.

Read Session One, "Inside Out: Expectations," in the leader guide and in the workbook. Review the steps in "Lead the Session," also in the leader guide.

Pray

Offer gratitude to God for insights, ideas, and guidance for the session. Give thanks for the group members and for what you will experience together.

Gather Materials and Set Up the Learning Area

- Bibles
- DVD, DVD player, and TV
- Leader guide
- Workbooks, have extras on hand for new members
- Nametags and markers/pens
- Chairs in a semicircle for viewing the video
- Small table covered with shiny fabric that suggests water
- Items that reflect water and journey themes, such as a small boat or a seashell
- A candle, basin, pitcher of water, and some smooth river stones (available at many craft supply stores) for the worship center
- A list on newsprint or poster paper of the Core Values on page 10 of the leader guide

Make sure that your meeting space is a comfortable area for discussion and reflection.

Set up and test the DVD equipment to make sure everything works properly.

Create a worship display in the center of the meeting area. Place the candle, basin, pitcher of water, stones, and the items that reflect water or a journey, on the cloth-covered table to create the worship center. Make sure to have at least one stone for each participant. The worship center should be the same in all the sessions.

Place the list of Core Values on a wall or other easily visible location in the learning area. This list of Core Values should remain on display through all the sessions.

On a wall or other location in the learning area that is easily visible to all participants, place a large sheet of paper with the quotation from Augustine of Hippo: "You have made us for yourself, and our heart is restless until it rests in you." This quotation should remain on display through all the sessions.

Lead the Session

Gathering and Opening Worship

Greet participants as they arrive. Invite them to make nametags and to find a place to sit.

The Stones and the Water (5 minutes)

In this exercise participants will be invited to begin this exploration of vocation with an act of worship incorporating water. While some of the class members may not have been baptized, baptismal imagery is central to Christian reflections on vocation; thus it is appropriate to begin here. The stone that is given to each participant during this opening exercise will be used later in the session as an invitation for class members to commit themselves to the Restless Hearts *Where Do I Go Now, God?* journey. For now the smooth river stones can be a mystery that participants hold in their hands as your discussion grows. The basin of water and stones can serve as your centering display for each session.

As participants arrive, ask them to choose a stone from the collection you have placed in the worship display area. Greet everyone and explain that you will start with a word of prayer over the water as a way of beginning this journey together.

In silence, slowly pour water into the bowl from the pitcher allowing participants to see and hear the water. After pouring, you may lift up some water in your hands and let it fall back into the basin.

This again emphasizes the importance of water as a symbol for this study. Offer aloud the following prayer, which is also in the workbook (page 14):

Bless to us, O God, this water—
from the waters of the womb
to journeys taken through stormy seas,
it is a reminder of your grace and promise.
Help us to walk with you.

Bless to us, O Christ, this group—
ready to explore and encounter
new callings and old.
Help us to walk with you.

Bless to us, Holy Spirit, this time—
ripe with potential
and full of your presence.
Help us to walk with you
as you walk with us. Amen.

Light the candle.

The Questions

View the Video (5–8 minutes)

Introduce the video segment as follows: "This video will help us explore the significance of restless hearts as the theme of the study."

View the video segment, "Introduction."

Ask the following questions:

- What thoughts or questions emerged as you watched "Introduction" on the DVD?
- What does restlessness suggest to you?
- What does it mean to you to rest in God?

Discuss Stories of Participants' Names (5 minutes)

One of the most unique things about us is our name. By inviting class members to share any stories they know related to their names, you provide a safe setting in which participants can begin to share. Also, you will set up the transition to the session topic and the Scripture passages.

Give each participant a workbook. Ask them to turn to page 14 and read the questions which ask:

- What do you know about how you got your name?
- What meaning does it hold for your family? For you?

Invite class members to share their responses to these questions with the group.

View the Video (5–8 minutes)

Introduce the first video segment as follows: "This video segment will help us to identify and reflect upon the tension between our inner sense of values and calling and the expectations that others have for us. Listening for God both inside and outside of ourselves is the lifelong process of vocation."

View the video segment, "Inside Out: Expectations."

Ask the following questions:

- What thoughts or questions emerged as you watched "Inside Out: Expectations" on the DVD?
- With which character in "The Wizard of Oz" do you identify most? Why?
- When have you felt tension between your own desires and expectations for what to do with your life and the expectations of others?

The Scriptures

The Bible contains several stories about significant births. Angelic visitors tell unsuspecting mothers that they will bear children who have some purpose that is known even before birth. Parents dedicate their children to a life of service to God before children have a chance to claim it on their own. These Bible study experiences invite participants to reflect on the kind of conflicts that might arise when a biblical character confronts the expectations imposed in this way. The exercise also asks class members to explore how these same dynamics might be operating in their lives.

Read and Discuss 1 Samuel 1:9-18; 3:1-21 and Judges 13:1-7, 24; 14:1-20 (8 minutes)

Introduce the exercise by talking about biblical stories of calling. Explain that many biblical characters are born into situations in which there is some promise or expectation attached to their birth. Isaac, John the Baptist, and Jesus are just some of the biblical figures who are children of promise. Tell participants that in this exercise they will be looking at two characters that dealt with the experience of being born into a story they didn't begin.

Have the participants break into two teams. Team One will read the story of Hannah, Eli, and Samuel (1 Samuel 1:9-18; 3:1-21) and the commentary about the Scripture in the workbook (page 18). Team Two will read the story of Samson and his parents (Judges 13:1-7, 24; 14:1-20) and the commentary about the Scripture in the workbook (pages 18–19). Have each team respond to the following questions in the workbook (page 19):

- To what is the child in each of these Scriptures committed before his birth?
- How does the child in each story respond to the expectations placed on him?
- Is there a conflict between the promise of the parent(s) and the will of the child? How do you see that at work in this story?

Develop a Skit (5 minutes)

As an additional option, have each team develop a brief skit imagining a conversation between Samson and his parents or between Samuel and Hannah. Ask the groups to be creative and to use their insights into the characters gained from the previous discussion. Have each group perform their skits. Following the skits, ask what new things participants learned from the presentations.

Discuss Psalm 139:16 (5 minutes)

Read aloud the following passage from Psalm 139:16: "Your eyes beheld my unformed substance./ In your book were written/ all the days that were formed for me." Explain that the psalmist was writing to express a belief that God was a constant presence even before birth. Invite the class members to reflect on this passage in connection with the skits they have just performed. Ask:

- What feelings arise as you read this passage and know that God and others see a purpose in your life?
- What might be restricting about these expectations?
- What might be liberating?

Your Life

Review Core Values List

Invite participants to look at the list of Core Values in the workbook (page 8) or posted in the learning area. Review these values. Tell the participants that they will be thinking about these values throughout the study. Every week they will be asked to reflect on these Core Values and how they inform the session topics. Encourage participants to continue this reflection by writing in the "Core Values and Your Life" box when they do their journaling in the workbook each week.

Explore a Core Value

In this exercise you will explore a key Core Value that underlies this course: *We are created to be related to God and others*. Participants will explore what this affirmation means to them and how it might affect their self-understanding in a world in which individualism often means downplaying the importance of key relationships.

Direct the attention of the group to the sheet with the quotation from Augustine, "You have made us for yourself, and our heart is restless until it rests in you." The quotation is also on page 21 of the workbook. Have someone read it aloud. Also remind them of the information about St. Augustine in the DVD and in the workbook. Invite participants to explain what the quotation means to them. Ask questions such as the following:

- To whom is this addressed?
- What does it mean to be "made for" something beyond yourself?
- In what ways is "restlessness" an appropriate word to describe your life? The world?
- What does it say to you about your relationship with God and others?

Read the Core Value "We are created to be related to God and others" in the workbook (page 8). Ask:

- What difference does the knowledge that we are created to be related make in how we live our lives and seek meaning?

Looking Ahead

Introduce the Workbook Discipline (5 minutes)

Explain that one of the major emphases of the Restless Hearts program is responding to questions in the workbook between sessions in order to help participants reflect on their vocational journey. The workbook is a resource for them to use in developing practices of prayer, reflection, and writing; and it will help them listen to God's voice in their journeys. Emphasize that their responses in the workbook can take many forms. Some may wish to write. Some may wish to draw or use symbols. Others may wish to use timelines. Some may even treat the workbook as a kind of scrapbook to collect pictures or items that are meaningful to them in responding to the exercise. Suggest that the weekly practice will be more effective if participants set aside time each day for reflection, even if it is only for a brief period (10–15 minutes). Participants may also want to try answering the questions multiple times to reflect new insights. Assure members that their workbook responses are their own and they will not have to share them with others unless they wish to do so.

Have the participants look at the boxes labeled "The Scriptures and Your Life" and "Core Values and Your Life." Tell them that they will be invited to write or draw responses in these boxes either during a session activity or on their own during the week between sessions.

Have the participants look at the questions in the "Looking Ahead" section in the workbook. Encourage them to respond to these questions each week.

Closing Worship

Casting Stones Into the Water

The closing act of worship allows participants to remember the symbolism of the baptismal water and to commit themselves to the Restless Hearts journey in the coming weeks. The stone placed in the water is a sign of their immersion into this supportive, exploring group. At the end of the last session, participants will be asked to retrieve a stone from the water to take with them as a visible reminder of their time in this group. The prayer time allows for a caring community to develop and for recognizing God's presence in the midst of our questioning and concerns.

Call the class to a time of worship by asking them to find the stone that they received at the beginning of the session. In your own words, introduce the worship act. You may say something like, "You may have been wondering what the stone you received was going to be used for. I want to suggest that you look at the stone as a symbol of your life. Reflecting on our vocations and lives is something that requires our whole selves. In a minute, we will have a period of silence in which we will pray for God's guidance in this journey.

During that silence I want to invite you to place your stone in the water as sign of your immersion in this journey of self-understanding. When we come to the end of this course in a few weeks time, we will retrieve a stone from the water."

Begin a period of silence with the words, "Let us pray." During the silence, participants can place their stones in the water. As leader, you should also place a stone in the water. Conclude the silence with the prayer printed in the workbook (page 23). Invite the participants to pray it in unison with you:

Spirit of life,
who blesses us with water and moves our restless hearts,
you have created us to be related
to you and to the world.
As we begin this journey together,
bless to us our lives
so that we can see patterns of purpose
and respond to your relentless tuggings
filled with grace and love.
Amen.

---

[1] From "XIII: Part Fourth of Baptism" in *The Large Catechism*, by Martin Luther, translated by F. Bente and W. H. T. Dau, in *Triglot Concordia: The Symbolical Books of the Evangelical Lutheran Church* (Concordia, 1921); accessible from: http://www.iclnet. org/pub/resources/text/wittenberg/luther/catechism/web/cat-13.html.

2

SESSION TWO
PASSION AND VOCATION

Focus:

The passions that drive us are often unacknowledged and some-times unappreciated. Uncovering what our hearts truly desire is one way to listen for God and to explore our vocation.

Objectives:

- To invite participants to listen to their passions as a way of lis-tening for God
- To affirm God's active presence in our inner lives
- To continue deepening the community within the study group

Reflections for This Session

Is it possible to get disconnected from your heart's desire? Obviously it is, because so many of us are lost in the quest to name that desire. I often think this disconnection is one of the primary things that separates human beings from the rest of God's cre-ation. No other creatures seem to become as tragically deluded as we do in living scripts that are so far from who we are meant to be. I doubt there are many sea anemones that struggle with uncovering their purpose in life. Duck-billed platypuses are not prone to mid-life crises. So we humans claim a unique role in the cosmos of forgetting who we are and, hopefully, reclaiming that knowledge in a moment or a lifetime of divine integration.

The Bible is full of affirmations that our lives are intended for something, and searching for the "something" is evident in the actions of biblical characters. Desire to be like God motivates the man and woman of the first garden. While this initial foray into vocational discernment did not end well, it was an early indicator that human beings would not be a contented people. In their restlessness they would search for meaning and purpose and occasionally, when they were open to God's Spirit moving within them and among them, they would find it and become part of God's story.

The passions of the human soul could prove to be unreliable guides when misdirected, just ask Samson and David. But these passions could also open up dimensions of human existence that lead to life. Even the graphic eroticism of Song of Solomon offers a window into the passion for God. Love really is "strong as death,/ passion fierce as the grave" (8:6).

Many young people in contemporary culture have been deceived into believing that our passions are not to be pulled out for public display because they may make us seem naïve and "out of synch" with the world around us. In campus ministry I often met with college students who kept their true desires and passions at arm's length because they felt no one would understand them if they revealed them. After long periods of repression, the heart's desires become like a once-loved teddy bear of childhood—something you might long for yet would not dare to take up again.

Psalm 65 offers a window into the desire of all creation for God. As fields and flocks and meadows overflow with joy, human beings are also invited to find their long-overdue shouts of praise. This session includes a passionate encounter with this text and invites participants to begin to explore those places that are waiting in silence within them. Giving voice to our passions may help us discern what is truly God and what is truly us.

Prepare for the Session

Let your preparation for the session be a time to pay attention to God and to the needs of group members as well as a time to review the content of the session. Find a quiet and comfortable place where you will not be interrupted. Have the DVD, a Bible, and the workbook available, in addition to the leader guide. Have paper and pen available to jot down notes, insights, and ideas. You may wish to keep these notes in a personal journal during this study.

Pray

Ask for God's guidance as you prepare for the session. Pray for the participants who will be a part of this session.

Read, View, and Reflect

As you read the leader guide, workbook, and Scriptures, and as you view the video segments, write down thoughts, insights, questions, and ideas that emerge for you. Also write questions that you think might emerge from the group.

Review the Core Values described in the introduction (page 10).

Read Psalm 65. Read the poem, "The Beat in the Silence," in the workbook (pages 27–30). Think about ways Psalm 65 and "The Beat in the Silence" relate to the focus for this session.

View the video segment, "Passion and Vocation."

Read Session Two, "Passion and Vocation," in the leader guide and in the workbook. Review the steps in "Lead the Session" in the leader guide.

Pray

Offer gratitude to God for insights, ideas, and guidance for the session. Give thanks for the group members and for what you will experience together.

Gather Materials and Set Up the Learning Area

- Bibles
- DVD, DVD player, and TV
- Leader guide
- Workbooks, have extras on hand for new members
- Nametags and markers/pens
- Chairs in a semicircle for viewing the video
- Small table covered with shiny fabric that suggests water
- Items that reflect water and journey themes, such as a small boat or a seashell
- A candle, basin, pitcher of water, and some smooth river stones (available at many craft supply stores) for the worship center
- A list on newsprint or poster paper of the Core Values (page 10)
- Slips of paper, pens/pencils, small container

Make sure that your meeting space is a comfortable area for discussion and reflection.

Set up and test the DVD equipment to make sure everything works properly.

Create a worship display in the center of the meeting area. Place the candle, basin, pitcher of water, stones, and the items that reflect water or a journey, on the cloth-covered table to create the worship center. Make sure there is one stone in the water for each participant. If new members join you for this session, be sure to have some extra smooth river stones available for them to use. Provide an opportunity for newcomers to place their stones in the basin at the end of opening worship. The worship center should be the same in all the sessions.

Place the list of Core Values on a wall or other location in the learning area that is easily visible to all participants. This list of Core Values should remain on display through all the sessions.

On a wall or other location in the learning area that is easily visible to all participants, place a large sheet of paper with the quotation from Augustine of Hippo: "For you have made us for yourself, and our heart is restless until it rests in you." Have this quotation on display through all the sessions.

Also on the wall, place a large sheet of paper with this quotation from Brian Mahan: "Vocation speaks of a gracious discovery of a kind of interior consonance between our deepest desires and hopes and our unique gifts, as they are summoned forth by the needs of others and realized in response to that summons."[1] Have this quotation on display for the remaining sessions.

Lead the Session

Gathering and Opening Worship

Greet participants as they arrive. Invite them to make nametags and to find a place to sit.

The Stones and the Water (5 minutes)

This exercise will draw participants back to the water as a reminder of where this vocational journey begins.

After participants have gathered, remind them of the exercise that closed the last session. Remind the group that each of the stones represents someone from the group and that the water reminds us of baptism as the sign of God's claim and promise for our lives. Give a stone to those who are new to the group. Invite the group to join you in a minute of silence, after which you will pour the water over the rocks in the basin. Invite participants to use the silence to remember someone who helped them understand something about God's work in their lives.

In silence, slowly pour the water into the bowl from the pitcher allowing participants to see and hear the water. Again, you may want to lift up some water in your hands and let it fall back into the basin. Pray together the following prayer, which can also be found in the workbook (page 26):

37

God of the deep, rich earth,
you were not afraid to get your hands dirty
in bringing us forth from the mud of the ground.
Help us to be grounded in your love.
Christ who went below the waters,
you were not afraid to immerse yourself
and to invite us to follow you in baptism.
Let your love flow in us.
Spirit of wind and flame,
you were not afraid to spark a fire
and to give your people voice and power.
Burn within us with your purifying love.
Amen.

Invite participants to dip their fingers in the water as you light the candle. Those who are new to the group may place their stones into the water at this time.

The Questions

View the Video (8–10 minutes)

Introduce the video segment as follows: "This video segment will help us to consider the passions that drive us, which are often unacknowledged and sometimes unappreciated. Uncovering what our hearts truly desire is one way to listen for God and to explore our vocation."

View the video segment, "Passion and Vocation."

Ask the following questions:

- What thoughts or questions emerged as you watched "Passion and Vocation" on the DVD?
- The people on the street named several passions: mission work, social justice, helping others. What other things are people passionate about?

38

• What connections do you see between a person's talents or skills and their passions?

Discuss and Define the Word "Passion" (3–5 minutes)

Have participants read the section "What Is Passion?" in the workbook (pages 26–27). Allow a few moments for them to write responses to the following questions that are also printed in the workbook:

- How do you define *passion*?
- What are you *passionate* about?
- What connections do you see between *passion* and *vocation*?

Discuss "The Beat in the Silence" (5–8 minutes)

Read the poem "The Beat in the Silence" from the workbook (pages 27–30). Ask the following questions that are also printed in the workbook:

- What images or ideas stand out for you in the poem?
- What does the idea of a beat in the silence suggest to you?
- What connections do you see between praise of God and passion?
- How does this poem speak to you about knowledge of self, of God, and of vocation?

The Scriptures

Introduce the biblical reading by explaining that we sometimes feel that we are not doing the most important things we should be doing. Psalm 65 talks about praise as the most natural language of creation. Ask participants to listen for what different parts of creation are doing in this psalm.

Read and Discuss Psalm 65 (8 minutes)

Have one person read Psalm 65 from his or her translation. Ask:

- What does God do in this psalm?
- What do the creatures and people do?
- What sort of relationship exists between God and the creation?
- What does this psalm say to you about passion and vocation?
- How does this psalm find expression in the poem, "The Beat in the Silence"?

Create a Responsive Reading of Psalm 65 (8–10 minutes)

If time allows, as an alternative or additional option have the group read the verses of Psalm 65 responsively as follows: Form two teams. Team One read the first verse. Team Two read the second verse. Team One read the third verse, and so on. Follow the responsive reading of the psalm with a discussion based on the above questions.

Review "Your Reflections on the Scriptures" (2 minutes)

Tell participants to respond to the question about Psalm 65 in the box labeled "Your Reflections on the Scriptures" (workbook, page 32) during the week. They may write or draw their responses.

Your Life

Discuss Childhood Dreams (10 minutes)

Our first hints of passion for a vocation come in our childhood fantasies of what we want to "be" when we grow up. This exercise will put participants in conversation with one another around those childhood dreams and the values that underlie them.

Introduce this segment by reminding participants of one of the questions they were asked to respond to in the journal through the week: "When you were a child, what did you want to be when you grew up?" Have each participant write down on a slip of paper his or her response to that question. Stress the importance of writing clearly because others will be reading it.

Put all of the responses in a container and then ask participants to draw one out making sure that the slip they keep is not their own. In a charade-like fashion (i.e. no words), have participants act out in turn the response they have drawn. Other group members will try to guess what is being communicated within a one-minute period. After the correct response is revealed, group members then have to guess who in the group wrote down that childhood dream. After everyone has had a turn, ask some follow-up questions:

- What made the dream you wrote down attractive to you as a child?
- How close do you feel to that childhood dream now?

Invite anyone who would like to share to tell about what they wrote in their journal during the past week. Do not pressure them to share if they are reticent.

Explore Vocation and Ambition (8 minutes)

In his book, *Forgetting Ourselves on Purpose*, Brian Mahan suggests that vocation and ambition play competing roles in our lives as we try to discover what it is that we are going to do and who it is that we are going to be. Ambition often implies a script that we must follow in order to succeed. Vocation, Mahan argues, is "unscripted."[2] In this exercise, group members will explore the difference between these concepts and respond to a quotation from Mahan.

Write the word "ambition" on the newsprint or white board. Invite participants to come add to the board a word or phrase that they associate with ambitious people. Alternatively, you could write the words and phrases as they are called out. After a time for response, evaluate what has been written. Ask:

- Do we seem to have a positive view or a negative view of ambition?
- How ambitious are your friends? The people you admire?

Introduce the concept of vocation. Say something like: "When we think of ambitious people we often think of someone who is hard-driving and directed toward a goal. Sometimes our ambitions are formed by our passions, but sometimes they cover them over. When we talk about vocation we talk about something that includes attention to these inner tuggings of our soul."

Have someone read the quotation from Brian Mahan, either from the sheet you have posted or from the workbook (page 33):

"Vocation speaks of a gracious discovery of a kind of interior consonance between our deepest desires and hopes and our unique gifts, as they are summoned forth by the needs of others and realized in response to that summons."

Ask participants to look at the quotation in the workbook and to underline words or phrases that speak to them. Ask the questions on page 33 of the workbook:

• What surprises you about this understanding of vocation?
• According to the quotation above, what things come together when we discover our vocation? What calls them forth?
• How is God speaking through this understanding of vocation?
• How are ambition and vocation different?

Review the Importance of Our Passions (5–8 minutes)

Introduce the next exercise by reviewing the different meanings of the word "passion" that you explored earlier in the session. On the newsprint or white board write the following open-ended sentence, which is also in the workbook (page 34): *Our passions are important because* _____. Invite participants to complete the sentence. Write the responses on the board.

Invite participants to draw a passion that is acting on them in the space provided on page 34 of the workbook. Tell members that they will not have to share their drawing with anyone else. Allow sufficient time for drawing. Discuss the following questions:

• What did you learn about your passion by drawing it?
• How can we listen for what God is saying in our passions? [Some possible responses: art, prayer, dreams, meditation, writing.]

42

Review Core Values List (5 minutes)

Invite participants to look at the list of Core Values in the workbook (page 8) or on the newsprint posted in the learning area. Ask, "Which of these Core Values speaks most to you about the topic of passion as we consider vocation?" Encourage participants to continue this reflection by writing in the Core Values box when they do their journal work in the workbook this week.

Looking Ahead

Discuss Journal Work (5 minutes)

This week the journal exercise encourages participants to catch themselves being themselves. In an exercise suggested by Brian Mahan, the participants will treat their journal as a "distraction diary" in which they write down stray thoughts that come to them as they are doing other things, for instance, while they are reading or sitting in class.[3]

Ask participants to turn to pages 36–37 of their student journals to read the journal exercise for the coming week. Have someone read the assignment aloud. Invite questions about the exercise, and encourage the group members again to take seriously the work they are doing between sessions, as you will be incorporating these reflections in the next session.

Remind the participants to respond to the questions in the boxes labeled "Your Reflections on the Scriptures" and "Core Values and Your Life."

Closing Worship

The Stones and the Water

In this closing prayer participants are asked to center themselves on a word that they have heard in this session.

Tell participants that you would like for them to think of one word that describes what God is doing within them. No other explanation will be required. Tell them that they will be sharing this word in the prayer that will follow a time of silence. Allow a minute of silent reflection. Encourage participants to write down the word they choose in their student journals on page 38. Ask group members to hold hands as you begin the prayer:

Spirit of life,
who blesses us with water and moves our restless hearts,
our passions burn within us.
Hear these words that sound in our souls:

[*Allow time for participants to reflect silently on their words. Share your word aloud and invite participants to do the same. Conclude the prayer:*]

For you praise waits in silence, God.
Let us join the chorus
and respond to your relentless tuggings
filled with joy.
Amen.

---

[1] *Forgetting Ourselves on Purpose: Vocation and the Ethics of Ambition,* by Brian J. Mahan (Jossey-Bass, 2002); pages 10–11.
[2] Mahan; page 10.
[3] Mahan; pages 34–37.

3

SESSION THREE
TRUSTING THE GIFTS

Focus:

Aptitude tests are a popular way for young people to begin to discern their gifts and abilities. Vocation moves us to a deeper level of trust that there is a purpose moving through our gifts. Such trust helps alleviate our anxieties about vocation.

Objectives:

- To allow participants to claim their gifts and abilities
- To encourage group members to trust that there is a purpose in their gifts
- To develop spiritual disciplines to discern God's activity in our journeys

Reflections for This Session

There are things about computers that I will never understand; and that is the reason I am always in awe of the computer-engineering students who were part of our campus ministry community at the University of Virginia. They seemed to have an uncanny gift and a useful, secret knowledge of the inner-workings of these complex machines we depend on so much. More amazing, however, was when those students discovered new "non-technical" gifts in the context of mission trips, Bible studies, and weekly student dinners. I felt I was always saying, "Look what those computer guys are doing now!"

Joel, a computer science graduate student, became a prophet that way. Always more practical than I was, Joel could take an important spiritual insight and turn it into inspired action. Once we took a mission trip over spring break to Yuma, Arizona. There, in the vast fields of lettuce growing out of the arid desert with the aid of massive irrigation that runs the Colorado River dry, we pledged to apply our Christian notions of justice to the production of our food supply.

It would all have remained very theoretical were it not for Joel's response. He came back to school and began a Saturday Local Foods Group that met early, went to the downtown farmer's market to buy locally-grown foods, improvised gourmet meals based on what was fresh, and made lunch together. I could talk a good game, but Joel was changing the world one delicious meal at a time and creating community as he did it! That was prophetic.

When young people claimed their gifts as a part of our ministry, it was always a powerful thing. I saw a first-year student transform a service project just by the insightful questions she began to ask about why we were there. I watched another engineering student blossom as a guitarist and worship leader. Another young woman came from the margins to the center of the community by making meals and making herself at home in a small group called Life 101. All of these students were expanding their worlds by finding God in newly-discovered gifts.

The next step was always more difficult, though. Having discerned what they *could* do, many students struggled with what they *should* do. Or to put it more dramatically, the question was, "What *must* I do given that I can do many things?" Many of the one-on-one sessions I held with students were variations on this theme, and I recall the deep struggle these young adults went through in answering that question.

The answer is usually not determined in an instant; more often it is a lifelong journey of understanding. Part of the journey is trusting that God is bound up in the ordering of our gifts and in the encouragement of our discernment. As one medieval Christian put it,

"Learn everything: you will afterwards discover that nothing is superfluous."[1] Once we find our direction, the pieces become part of a greater whole.

Steve Jobs, CEO of Apple Computer, Inc., and Pixar Animation Studios, told a graduating class of college students that he was forever grateful for the opportunity to take a class that at the time seemed absolutely impractical. In a calligraphy class, he learned about typefaces, fonts, and spacing, which he appreciated because of their inherent beauty. It was only ten years later, as he was designing the now-famous Macintosh computer, that the importance of that class became clear. What made the Macintosh stand out was the attention it gave to fonts and type, something that could only have happened because Jobs took calligraphy. "You can't connect the dots looking forward," Jobs told the graduates, "you can only connect them looking backwards. So you have to trust that the dots will somehow connect in your future. You have to trust in something."[2]

Trusting is a discipline that must be cultivated. In this session, class participants will be invited to confront the storm of confusion and fear that can mark our vocational journey. They will also be invited to trust that in their gifts and in God's promise there is a purpose for them. We will also explore spiritual exercises to help us develop that trust.

Prepare for the Session

Let your preparation for the session be a time to pay attention to God and to the needs of group members as well as a time to review the content of the session. Find a quiet and comfortable place where you will not be interrupted. Have the DVD, a Bible, and the workbook available, in addition to the leader guide. Have paper and pen available to jot down notes, insights, and ideas. You may wish to keep these notes in a personal journal during this study.

Pray

Ask for God's guidance as you prepare for the session. Pray for the participants who will be a part of this session.

Read, View, and Reflect

As you read the leader guide, workbook, and Scriptures, and as you view the video segments, write down thoughts, insights, questions, and ideas that emerge for you. Also write questions that you think might emerge from the group.

Review the Core Values described in the introduction (page 10).

Read Luke 10:38-42. Read "Vera and the Storm" in the workbook (pages 40–42). Think about ways Luke 10:38-42 and "Vera and the Storm" relate to the focus for this session.

View the video segment, "Trusting the Gifts."

Read Session Three, "Trusting the Gifts," in the leader guide and in the workbook. Review the steps in "Lead the Session" in the leader guide.

Read the section about breath prayers in "Breathing In, Breathing Out" (workbook, page 49). Read the closing worship section on pages 55–57 of the leader guide. Practice the spiritual discipline of the breath prayer before the group meets.

Pray

Offer gratitude to God for insights, ideas, and guidance for the session. Give thanks for the group members and for what you will experience together.

Gather Materials and Set Up the Learning Area

- Bibles
- DVD, DVD player, and TV
- Leader guide
- Workbooks, have extras on sale for new members
- Nametags and markers or pens
- Chairs in a semicircle for viewing the video
- Small table covered with shiny fabric that suggests water
- Items that reflect water and journey themes, such as a small boat or a seashell

- A candle, basin, pitcher of water and some smooth river stones (available at many craft supply stores) for the worship center
- A list on newsprint or poster paper of the Core Values on page 10 of the leader guide

Make sure that your meeting space is a comfortable area for discussion and reflection.

Set up and test the DVD equipment to make sure everything works properly.

Create a worship display in the center of the meeting area. Place the candle, basin, pitcher of water, stones, and the items that reflect water or a journey, on the cloth-covered table to create the worship center. Make sure there is one stone in the water for each participant. If new members join you for this session, be sure to have some extra smooth river stones available for them to use. Provide an opportunity for newcomers to place their stones in the basin at the end of opening worship. The worship center should be the same in all the sessions.

Place the list of Core Values on a wall or other easily visible location in the learning area. This list of Core Values should remain on display through all the sessions.

Lead the Session

Gathering and Opening Worship

Greet participants as they arrive. Invite them to make nametags and to find a place to sit.

The Stones and the Water (5 minutes)

This opening time of worship centers once again on the water but connects with the work students have been doing in their journals. By encouraging attention to distractions and to where our minds wander when encountering evocative sounds and symbols, we deepen the experience of the God who operates in every part of our lives.

Lift the pitcher of water in your hands and explain to the group what you are about to do. Tell them that they should close their eyes and listen as you pour the water over the rocks in the basin. Share that they will hear water falling in a basin but they may also hear other times when they have heard water. Perhaps they will recall the sound of a bath being drawn, a baby being baptized, or a leaky faucet. They may be distracted by these other times when they have noticed the sound of water, but this time they should pay attention to the distractions and let those other images of water come into their minds. Tell the group that you will ask them to share what they hear in a moment.

In silence, slowly pour the water into the bowl from the pitcher allowing participants to hear the water. After pouring it in, lift up some water in your hands and let it fall back into the basin.

With eyes still closed, invite group members to share the images they have experienced while listening to the water.

Pray together this prayer which is found on page 40 of the workbook:

God of migrant wanderers,
our minds drift and slip and flow
from passionate awareness of your presence
to forgetfulness and fear.
Bless to us this day our lives
that we may follow where Abraham and Sarah once did,
out from the comfortable places where we hang out
to the new territories where we can live
with you.
Amen.

Invite participants to dip their fingers in the water as you light the candle. Those who are new to the group may place their stones into the water at this time.

The Questions

View the Video (8–10 minutes)

Introduce the video segment as follows: "This video segment will help us to acknowledge our gifts and abilities and to trust more deeply that there is a purpose moving through our gifts."

View the video segment, "Trusting the Gifts."

Ask the following questions:

- What thoughts or questions emerged as you watched "Trusting the Gifts" on the DVD?
- When have you experienced a "storm" as you thought about your vocation? What was it like?
- What are some of the stresses you experience when you think about your vocation?
- How did you respond to the story about Steve Jobs and the image of connecting the dots?

Review Journal Work—"Driven by Distraction" (5 minutes)

The journal exercise for the week asked participants to pay attention to those things that we usually ignore or try to put out of our minds. This exercise encouraged us to see how God may be speaking to us even in these moments. This segment of the lesson should encourage sharing among class members. Be attentive to involving everyone in the discussion.

Ask participants to turn in their workbooks to page 36 where they have written responses to the question: "What I'm really thinking about is . . ."

Use the following questions to guide your discussion:

- In what situations did you find yourself most distracted this week?
- What surprised you about what you were thinking in those moments?
- Where was God speaking to you in your distractions?

- If you paid more attention to your stray thoughts, what might you change about what you are doing now?

Discuss "Vera and the Storm" (10 minutes)

Select three persons to read the story "Vera and the Storm" in the workbook (pages 40–42). One person will read as a narrator, another as Vera, and another as Gabriella. After the reading, discuss the following questions that are also printed in the workbook:

- What is making Vera anxious in the story?
- How does Gabriella respond to her? With whom do you most identify, Vera or Gabriella? Why?
- How does the storm reflect Vera's mood?
- Does being away from home or being in a storm describe your feelings about vocation? Why or why not?

The Scriptures

Read and Discuss Martha and Mary in Luke 10:38-42 (8 minutes)

The story of Martha and Mary appears in the Gospel of Luke. The story gives insights about both gifts and anxiety. Martha is easily caricatured in this passage as someone who busies herself in service while neglecting to hear Jesus' message. But Jesus chides her, not for her service, but for her anxiety. His focus is on what is most important in the midst of the many things that could be happening. In this Bible study exercise, group members will imagine themselves as Martha and Mary and reflect on what is most important for them to hear in the midst of our contemporary world.

Ask participants to turn in their Bibles to Luke 10:38-42. This passage is also printed on page 43 of the workbook. Ask three volunteers to read the passage with each taking a different role: narrator, Martha, and Jesus. The passage is marked in this way in the workbook.

Explore the passage by asking class members to imagine themselves as Martha and Mary being interviewed following Jesus' departure. Divide the class into two groups and have one group respond to the following questions as Martha and one group as Mary.

- What was your response when you realized that Jesus was coming to your house?
- What did you hear Jesus saying to you while he was here?

Bring the groups back together and have them share their responses to the questions.

Review "Your Reflections on the Scriptures" (2 minutes)

Tell participants to respond to the questions about Luke 10:38-42 in the box labeled "Your Reflections on the Scriptures" (workbook, page 44) during the week. They may write or draw their responses.

Your Life

Do the Tree and the Wind Activity (10 minutes)

In this exercise participants will explore their own feelings of trust and how they see trust at work in their own lives.[3]

Have participants stand in a tight circle, shoulder to shoulder. Ask a volunteer to stand in the middle of the circle. [If you have group members who are not physically able to participate in this activity, see the alternative activity on the next page.]

Explain that in this exercise we will be simulating a tree being blown in the wind. The person in the center of the circle will cross their arms across their chest and imagine that they are rooted in place like a great willow. They should close their eyes throughout the exercise. As the wind begins to blow they will start to sway without moving their feet. To prevent the tree from falling, those in the circle will gently push the tree back toward the center. After the initial sway, the tree should fall naturally in the direction it is pushed.

Begin the exercise and continue until all the group members have had a chance to be in the center.

Evaluate the game by using the following questions:

• How did you feel when you were the tree?
• How did you feel when you were the wind?
• What made this exercise difficult?

Ask group members to turn to page 45 in their workbooks and respond to the questions under "The Tree and the Wind." Tell them to take their feelings from the exercise and to imagine that the tree and the wind represent parts of themselves.

Invite participants to talk about insights they gained from the exercise.

Alternative Exercise:

If there are persons in your group who would find the exercise above difficult, you may adapt the game by doing the game as a guided meditation. Ask participants to close their eyes and to imagine with you the following scene. If you have some soft music that evokes images of a gentle breeze, you could play that in the background as you read. Be sure to read slowly and clearly to allow participants to enter the scene:

Imagine that you are a willow tree standing tall and billowing on a hill-side. It is a bright summer day and there is a slight breeze blowing your long, thin branches. You have a strong trunk that is rooted deeply in the earth. Feel how stable the ground is beneath you, supporting your great height. Feel how soft the breeze is as it rustles your beautiful leaves. [Pause.]

Now on the horizon a dark cloud appears, and as it grows closer you feel the wind growing stronger and stronger. What seemed gentle and light now feels fierce and overwhelming. You bend much further than you think you can without breaking in two. You feel your roots straining against the earth. You wonder if you can hold yourself up. [Pause.]

But you know that you are planted deeply in the ground. You know your trunk is strong. You remember the storms that you have weathered before. The wind dies down again and you are still there on the hillside, waiting for the sun to return.

Ask group members to respond to the exercise by sharing thoughts or feelings they had during the meditation.

Review Core Values List (5 minutes)

Invite participants to look at the list of Core Values in the workbook (page 8) or on the newsprint posted in the learning area. Ask, "Which of these Core Values speak most to you about trusting that God has a purpose for your gifts? About your anxieties related to vocation?" Encourage participants to continue this reflection by writing in the Core Values box when they do their journal work in the workbook this week.

Looking Ahead

Discuss Journal Work—"The Parts That Need Changing" (5 minutes)

In this exercise, class members will be creating a spiritual autobiography with an eye on the necessary changes that need to happen for growth to occur.

- Ask participants to turn to page 47 of their workbooks to read the journal exercise for the coming week. Have someone read the assignment aloud.
- Invite questions about the exercise and encourage the group members again to take seriously the work they are doing between sessions, as you will be incorporating these reflections in the next session.
- Remind the participants to respond to the questions in the boxes labeled "Your Reflections on the Scriptures" and "Core Values and Your Life."

Closing Worship

Breathing In, Breathing Out (5 minutes)

This exercise uses a phrase inspired by Luke 10:41-42 as an introduction to "breath prayers" as a spiritual exercise. Participants will be encouraged to continue using this prayer through the coming week. As leader, you should spend some time before the session, practicing this type of prayer so that you can lead this exercise.

Explain that for the closing prayer you will be using a form of prayer called the breath prayer. Share with the class that this is a very old form of Christian prayer that desert mystics used for centering and meditating. By calming ourselves, listening for God's voice, and repeating a very simple prayer phrase, we deepen our trust in God's presence. Explain that this closing prayer exercise is one spiritual discipline that class members can use along with their journaling. Encourage them to try it out in the coming week.

If it is possible, dim the lights in your room so that the candlelight is the primary source of light. Ask group members to make themselves comfortable in their seats and to close their eyes. Invite them to hold their hands open with palms facing upwards as a sign of receptivity to the Holy Spirit.

Have participants concentrate on their breathing, paying attention to the rise and fall of their breath. Tell them to inhale deeply and slowly and then to exhale in the same way. Ask them to repeat this for several more seconds.

Now ask group members to whisper the following prayer as they breathe in: "Jesus, lover of my soul." Then have them whisper, "You alone are all I need" as they breathe out. Ask them to feel the rhythm of the words as they breathe in and out and to repeat them. Explain that they may find their minds drifting to other things as they pray. When that happens, they should acknowledge the thought and offer it to God, returning to the words they are saying as they breathe.

After several minutes, invite participants once again to become aware of the sound of their breath. Ask them to open their eyes slowly as you turn the lights back on.

Conclude the session by praying the following prayer, which is printed on page 49 of the workbook:

Jesus, Lover of our souls,
you call us from the craziness of our days
to discover the one thing we need to live.
As the men and women who were your disciples
left behind what they knew
to become what they would be,
so let us walk in your way,
share in your joy,
and dance in your love.
Amen.

---

[1] These words of Hugh of St. Victor are found in *A History of Medieval Philosophy*, by F. C. Copleston (University of Notre Dame Press, 1972); page 95.

[2] The text of the Stanford Commencement address given by Steve Jobs, June 12, 2005, can be found on the Stanford University website at: http://news-service.stanford.edu/news/2005/june15/jobs-061505.html.

[3] For introducing me to this exercise, I am indebted to *More New Games!*, by Andrew Fluegelman (Doubleday, 1981); page 67.

4

SESSION FOUR
LISTENING IN THE SHADOWS

Focus:

Once we accept that we are on a vocational journey oriented toward God, we may come to despise or suppress those parts of us that we feel are unworthy or unnecessary. However, there are treasures to be found when we search among our needs, anxieties, and places of brokenness for God's healing presence.

Objectives:

- To explore the role that our "shadow side" plays in helping us listen for God
- To initiate the development of symbols of who or what God is calling participants to be
- To introduce confession and healing as disciplines drawing us to wholeness

Reflections for This Session

Job's friends have a notoriously bad reputation for giving advice. Most readers of the biblical reflection on human suffering come away feeling that the reputation is well-deserved. After all, Job is afflicted with the worst calamities that could be imagined in his day and their general response seems to be, "Gee, Job, you must have done something really wrong to deserve this."

But there is a bit of counsel offered by one of the friends that has the ring of real insight. Late in the book a previously silent friend, Elihu, responds to Job's accusation that God was not speaking to offer answers to Job's questions. Elihu observes that perhaps God *is* speaking to Job in ways he cannot discern (Job 33:14-30). In his suffering and in his dreams, God was giving Job new messages to guide him on his way. Job never gets a chance to respond to Elihu because God shows up in a whirlwind immediately after his speech; but Jews and Christians in the centuries following have sometimes heeded Elihu, listening for God in the shadows, attending to the ways God speaks in our brokenness and whispers in our dreams.

Pivotal moments in healing often come through the ministrations of dreams. In our nightly visions, God presents us with images whose symbolic power opens new avenues for growth. Often these images lead us to unresolved wounds or unrecognized needs that are crying out for attention. Because we do not acknowledge these places in our waking life, they work below the surface, rippling through our lives with sometimes surprising consequences.

When my grandmother died, I had a series of dreams in which I saw through a doorway a bed on which my grandmother was lying. For weeks I could only see her feet and when I would approach the doorway, I would hear her voice saying, "Not yet. I'm not ready yet." It was months later that I finally had a dream in which I saw her face and then the setting had changed. She was back in her home doing what she loved. The dreams mirrored my grieving as I moved from disorientation and a sense of being disconnected from someone who grounded me (a role that feet also have!) to a fuller acceptance of my grandmother's joy still being present in my life.

The vocational journey is not a linear path that moves from recognition of gifts to employment and enjoyment of them. When we are at our best, we acknowledge the revelatory power of our shadow side as well. In our needs, anxieties, wounds, and frustrations are the seeds of new journeys and new healing. A healthy pattern of confession can help us continually to keep ourselves open to the places God needs to work in our lives.

Young adults in the post-*Seinfeld* generation are no strangers to acknowledging the sides of ourselves that are less than pretty. Fed a steady diet of media characters like Jerry and Elaine, who possess their own flaws but laugh at those of others, there is a certain protection from ridicule that comes with admitting your faults before others can. But there are all too few safe places to take our ailing selves for healing.

In this session, class members will head into the shadows to see where God is at work. As they do, they will be invited to see the role of confession and healing as Christian practices leading to a deeper experience of God and a deeper understanding of themselves.

Prepare for the Session

Let your preparation for the session be a time to pay attention to God and to the needs of group members as well as a time to review the content of the session. Find a quiet and comfortable place where you will not be interrupted. Have the DVD, a Bible, and the workbook available, in addition to the leader guide. Have paper and pen available to jot down notes, insights, and ideas. You may wish to keep these notes in a personal journal during this study.

Pray

Ask for God's guidance as you prepare for the session. Pray for the participants who will be a part of this session.

Read, View, and Reflect

As you read the leader guide, workbook, and Scriptures, and as you view the video segments, write down thoughts, insights, questions, and ideas that emerge for you. Also write questions that you think might emerge from the group.

Review the Core Values described in the introduction (page 10).

Read Luke 13:10-17, the story of the bent-over woman. Read "I Have to Take This Call" on pages 52–54 in the workbook. Think about ways Luke 13:10-17 and "I Have to Take This Call" relate to the focus for this session.

View the video segment, "Listening in the Shadows."

Read Session Four, "Listening in the Shadows," in the leader guide and in the workbook. Review the steps in "Lead the Session" in the leader guide.

Read the activities suggested for the journal exercise "Moving Out." Spend some time investigating possible places where class members can engage in service and/or justice ministries.

As leader you may want to spend some time in the week before the session reflecting on how you have experienced God at work in you healing wounds and addressing needs. Ask yourself how these times helped you to grow in understanding God and yourself. You may also want to keep a dream journal through the week to help you identify with the symbolic world of your dreams.

Pray

Offer gratitude to God for insights, ideas, and guidance for the session. Give thanks for the group members and for what you will experience together.

Gather Materials and Set Up the Learning Area

- Bibles
- DVD, DVD player, and TV
- Leader guide
- Workbooks, have extras on hand for new members
- Nametags and markers or pens
- Chairs in a semicircle for viewing the video
- Small table covered with shiny fabric that suggests water
- Items that reflect water and journey themes, such as a small boat or a spiraling seashell
- A candle, basin, pitcher of water, and some smooth river stones (available at many craft supply stores) for the worship center
- Lumps of modeling clay
- Table(s) for working with clay

- Moist towelettes for cleaning hands
- Pipe cleaners
- Poster or newsprint with the following sentence written on it: "Don't invite God in if you don't want to change."

Make sure that your meeting space is a comfortable area for discussion and reflection.

Set up and test the DVD equipment to make sure everything works properly.

Create a worship display in the center of the meeting area. Place items that reflect water or a journey, the candle, basin, pitcher of water, and stones on the cloth-covered table to create the worship center. Make sure there is one stone in the water for each participant. If new members join you for this session, be sure to have some extra smooth river stones available for them to use. Provide an opportunity for newcomers to place their stones in the basin at the end of opening worship. The worship center should be the same in all the sessions.

Have a one or more tables available for working with the clay. Place lumps of clay on the table(s) ahead of time.

Place the list of Core Values on a wall or other location in the learning area that is easily visible to all participants. This list of Core Values should remain on display through all the sessions.

Place the poster with the phrase, "Don't invite God in if you don't want to change," on a wall or other location that is easily visible to all participants.

Lead the Session

Gathering and Opening Worship

Greet participants as they arrive. Invite them to make nametags and to find a place to sit.

The Stones and the Water (5 minutes)
This exercise will draw participants back to the water as a reminder of where this vocational journey begins.

Welcome class members and invite them to enter into worship by closing their eyes and concentrating on their breathing. If you can dim the lighting in the room, do so now.

Recalling the breath prayer from the last session, ask them to repeat the following phrase as they breathe in: "Spirit, moving in my soul. . ." As they breathe out, they should whisper, "Wash me, cleanse me, make me whole."

As class members continue the breath prayer, slowly pour the water into the bowl from the pitcher. After pouring it in, lift up some water in your hands and let it fall back into the basin.

Have participants slowly open their eyes and then raise the lighting if you have dimmed it.

Pray together this prayer which is found on page 52 of the student journal:

Spirit, moving in my soul,
you uncover my thoughts
and trouble my self-deceptions.
Disturb me
like a field is prepared for planting
and open my heart to grow.
Spirit, moving in my soul,
wash me,
cleanse me,
make me whole. Amen.

Invite participants to dip their fingers in the water as you light the candle.

The Questions

View the Video (8–10 minutes)

Introduce the video segment as follows: "This video segment will help us to consider the treasures to be found when we search among our needs, anxieties, and places of brokenness for God's healing presence."

View the video segment, "Listening in the Shadows."

Ask the following questions:

- What thoughts or questions emerged as you watched "Listening in the Shadows" on the DVD?
- What are the shadows in your life?
- What did you learn or what might you learn from your shadows?

Discuss "I Have to Take This Call" (10 minutes)

Read the story "I Have to Take This Call" (workbook, pages 52–54).

Ask the following questions to stimulate discussion. Remind participants that they do not have to talk about personal responses they may have written in their workbooks unless they want to talk about them.

- What is your response to the different boxes in the young man's closet?
- Which box best describes what is in your closet? Why?
- In the story, we hear only the young man's side of the conversation. What do you think God says to him as he responds to the affirmations on each of the boxes?
- What connections do you make between the metaphor of the closet with its storage boxes and the topic of listening to God in the shadows?

The Scriptures

Read and Discuss Luke 13:10-17, the Story of the Bent-over Woman

Introduce this activity and discussion by explaining that sometimes the healing stories in the Bible give us powerful images of how God transforms lives. The story of the bent-over woman is one such story. It demonstrates the effects of unacknowledged burdens and the transformation that God's healing can bring about. This exercise includes a physical activity. If persons in your group are living with a disability, you may wish to do this exercise by inviting participants to imagine the postures rather than to actually do them.

Ask a volunteer to read Luke 13:10-17 from his or her Bible.

Ask class members to stand and bend over so that they are staring at the floor. If there are persons in your group who are unable to stand, ask them to stare at the floor from their seated position. Ask them to respond to the following questions while they remain in this position:

- If this were how you had lived for 18 years, what things would you be more likely to notice?
- How might you think of yourself?

Now ask participants to stand up straight (or look up if they are seated). Ask them to respond to the following question while they remain in this position:

- If this were the first time you looked straight ahead in 18 years, how would you feel? What would you be likely to notice?

Invite participants to be seated and to imagine themselves as the others in the synagogue who challenged Jesus for curing the woman. Ask:

- What might be threatening to you about having this woman stand up and begin to praise God?
- Why are you more interested in upholding the rules than allowing healing to happen?

Conclude by asking:

- With which character do you identify most—the bent-over woman, the healed woman, the rule-keepers, or someone else in the story? Why?

Review "Your Reflections on the Scriptures" (2 minutes)

Tell participants to respond to the question about Luke 13:10-17 in the box labeled "Your Reflections on the Scriptures" during the week. They may write or draw their responses.

Your Life

Review Journal Work—"My Spiritual Autobiography" (5 minutes)

The journal assignment for this week asked class members to construct a spiritual autobiography and to identify places within themselves that changed at the time of marker events. This exercise allows participants to share insights gained from the journal exercise. Remind participants that they do not have to talk about their insights unless they wish to do so.

Ask participants to turn to page 47 in their student journals where they were asked for their responses to the spiritual autobiography exercise.

Invite reflection on the exercise by asking the following questions of the group:

- What was one new thing you learned about yourself as a result of this exercise?
- What had to change in you in those moments when you grew closer to God?
- If you had to choose one area of your life to give to God for some "extra work," what would you choose?

Additional Exercise:

If you have more time for this exercise you can deepen the experience of the spiritual autobiography by giving each participant a pipe cleaner. Ask them to imagine that the length of the pipe cleaner is a timeline stretching from their birth to their current age. Participants should mark key events in their relationship with God by bending the pipe cleaner at appropriate points. (E.g. a person might bend the pipe cleaner upward to mark an important experience at a church camp or bend it downward to mark the death of a parent.) After allowing time for class members to complete the exercise, invite sharing around the question:

- What does one of the major bends in your pipe cleaner represent?

Continue with the questions listed on the previous page.

Create Clay Sculptures (10 minutes)

Introduce the clay exercise by saying that we all have places in our lives that feel vulnerable or wounded. When we allow God to meet us in these places for healing, we are freer to respond to our vocation. Invite participants to use the clay on the tables to mold a symbol of some part of themselves they know needs to be changed or healed. Assure class members that you will not ask them to share this symbol and that their work is their own.

When clay sculptures are finished, pass around the moist towelettes as you ask:

- What did you feel as you created this symbol of something you may have kept secret?

Tell participants that you will be returning to this sculpted clay later in the session.

Review Core Values List (5 minutes)

Invite participants to look at the list of Core Values in the workbook (page 8) or on the newsprint posted in the learning area. Ask: Which of these Core Values speak most to you about listening to God in the shadows and experiencing God's transformation? Encourage them to continue this reflection by writing in the Core Values box when they do their journal work this week.

Looking Ahead

Discuss Journal Work—"Moving Out" (5 minutes)

In the coming week the journal exercise invites participants to get involved with an activity that helps others. The work we have done so far in this study focuses on how we experience vocation internally. Now we want to explore how interaction with the needs of the world can call forth our heart's desire. Some of the class participants may already be involved in service activities, but those who are not may need some help in identifying how they can carry out this exercise. Spend some time preparing a list of possible sites for service work in the coming week. You may want to consider organizing an activity as a class. Possibilities include: reading to children in an elementary school, participating in home repair or home construction with non-profit groups, volunteering at a food kitchen, gleaning fields for the food bank, and doing field work for a community organizing group. This exercise is much more effective if participants reflect on an activity they have done very recently. While the journal exercise allows for reflection on past work, strongly encourage class members to do something this week.

Ask participants to turn to pages 60–61 of their workbooks to read the journal exercise for the coming week. Have someone read the assignment out loud.

If you have prepared a list of possible service sites and activities, share it with the group. If you are planning a group activity, share details and what participants should expect.

Invite questions about the exercise. Encourage group members to participate in an activity this week rather than relying on past experiences.

Remind the participants to respond to the questions in the boxes labeled "Your Reflections on the Scriptures" and "Core Values and Your Life."

Closing Worship

Remold Me, Make Me

Here class members return to the sculpted clay from the earlier exercise and transform it into a symbol of healing. This becomes part of a closing worship experience that introduces confession and healing as ways God brings about wholeness.

Ask class members to retrieve their clay sculptures from the earlier exercise. Remind them that the sculptures were meant to represent a part of themselves that needed to be changed or healed. Tell them that in this closing worship exercise they will transform the clay into a new symbol.

Tell the class members to look at their creations as they reflect on what they hope God would change. Remind them that change means that what they have created will have to be redone. Ask them to think about how they will remold their work. Will they gently rework the clay building from the shape that is there? Will they smash it into a formless blob and begin all over again? What sort of change is required in their lives?

Ask the group to work in silence now, remolding their clay into a symbol of the healing they would like to experience. Give them ten minutes to complete the project.

Have the group clean their hands.

Invite anyone who would like to share his or her creation to do so briefly.

Ask each member to think of one verb that expresses what God is doing in their lives at the moment. Examples might be: waiting, churning, cultivating, or burning. Go around the circle and share the verbs.

Point out the sentence on the newsprint in your room: "Don't invite God in if you don't want to change." Point out that the clay exercise might be considered an act of confession—opening up parts of our lives that we usually keep hidden so that God can change and heal us. Stress that Christians sometimes think that confession is about feeling bad for what we have done. Confession has more to do with opening ourselves to what God can do even in those places we consider weak. Encourage group members to continue a discipline of daily confession.

Have group members turn to page 61 in the student journal and read the prayer printed there together:

Spirit, moving in my soul,
I open my hands
and know they are scarred.
I open my eyes
and know they often stray.
I open my heart
and know it can love more.
I open my life
and ask you to come in.
Remold me.
Make me yours. Amen.

5

SESSION FIVE
SOMEBODY'S CALLING YOUR NAME

Focus:

We have affirmed that looking inward helps us discern vocation because God is active and at work in our history, our gifts, and even our flaws. However, we can also claim our vocation as we meet God in the needs of the world.

Objectives:

- To encourage participants to develop a pattern of engaging in acts of service and justice
- To identify needs in the world around us that are crying out for response
- To allow participants to formulate expressions of vocation in relation to the call they are experiencing from their environment

Reflections for This Session

Frederick Buechner, the venerable Presbyterian sage, is justly credited with giving language to many vocational crises. His introspective manner and willingness to share deeply from his personal story in his many writings resonate with many pilgrims seeking their place in God's world. One of his most quoted lines is a definition of vocation:

"The place God calls you to is the place where your deep gladness and the world's deep hunger meet."[1]

Like many things that have been said many times, it is a definition that invites periodic reevaluation. Is it really true that we can experience a consonance between our internal journey and the needs of the world? Or does Buechner imply, as I suspect, something with a bit more tension? The meeting of deep gladness and deep hunger is not always a happy one, but it is certainly a necessary one.

Once I attended a conference full of clergy people who came together because they had a concern for clergy recruitment. One of the exercises our table engaged in was a sharing of our own stories of call into ministry. As we worked our way around the group, there were many tales of anguished nights of soul-searching, moments of great personal conviction when it suddenly became clear that God had a hand on the individual, and passages into ordained ministry that were marked by struggles and assurance. My own story had hints of these themes. The call to ministry was a quest, and we had finally yielded to its urgency.

But the last person to share was a colleague of mine who did not talk about finding her calling deep within. She had seen people who were struggling and in great need, and she determined that God would give her what she needed to help them. To use Buechner's language, while most of us around the table were intent on discovering the deep gladness of our souls, the deep hunger of her people moved her.

Campus ministers know that some of the highlights of every program year are the mission experiences. When students leave behind their school environment for a time, particularly when they are involved in cross-cultural journeys, they often discover that God is speaking to them in ways they never expected. I began to listen carefully to student reflections when we were on these trips.

On a journey to the border region of South Texas one year, a student told me, in an off-handed way, that she could see herself working on the border on migrant issues. In an instant, I could see that such a course was indeed likely for her. She had an interest in justice, in international relations, and in the welfare of people living on the margins. I don't remember what I said to her, but I do remember encouraging and affirming her vision. A few years later, she was doing exactly what she had dreamed on that trip, working with a border ministry in Arizona.

So far in this study we have been delving deeply into the conscious and unconscious internal movements of our souls to try to listen for God's activity. In this session, we move out into a world that is also alive with God's Spirit. As participants develop attentiveness to the world's deep hungers, they may also find a word for their own journeys.

Prepare for the Session

Let your preparation for the session be a time to pay attention to God and to the needs of group members as well as a time to review the content of the session. Find a quiet and comfortable place where you will not be interrupted. Have the DVD, a Bible, and the workbook available, in addition to the leader guide. Have paper and pen available to jot down notes, insights, and ideas. You may wish to keep these notes in a personal journal during this study.

Pray

Ask for God's guidance as you prepare for the session. Pray for the participants who will be a part of this session. Reflect on how you have met God in others and in the needs of the world. Undertake the activity suggested for the students in the journal this week. As you participate in service and/or justice activities, reflect on the roles these have played in your own vocational journey.

Read, View, and Reflect

As you read the leader guide, workbook, and Scriptures, and as you view the video segments, write down thoughts, insights, questions, and ideas that emerge for you. Also write questions that you think might emerge from the group.

Review the Core Values described in the introduction (page 10).

Read Isaiah 58 and Matthew 25:31-46. Read "I Want to Hear My True Name" on pages 64–66 in the workbook. Think about ways Isaiah 58, Matthew 25:31-46, and "I Want to Hear My True Name" relate to the focus for this session.

View the video segment, "Somebody's Calling Your Name."

Read Session Five, "Somebody's Calling Your Name," in this leader guide and in the workbook. Review the steps in "Lead the Session" in the leader guide.

Pray

Offer gratitude to God for insights, ideas, and guidance for the session. Give thanks for the group members and for what you will experience together.

Gather Materials and Set Up the Learning Area

- Bibles
- DVD, DVD player, and TV
- Leader guide
- Workbooks, have extras on hand for new members
- Nametags and markers or pens
- Chairs in a semicircle for viewing the video
- Small table covered with shiny fabric that suggests water
- Items that reflect water and journey themes, such as a small boat or a spiraling seashell
- A candle, basin, pitcher of water and some smooth river stones (available at many craft supply stores) for the worship center
- Large sheet of newsprint or poster paper with the following sentence: "Vocation is a hands-on activity."
- Collage supplies: glue, scissors, poster board, and newspaper or magazine pictures depicting situations and people that may be calling us to act

Make sure that your meeting space is a comfortable area for discussion and reflection.

Set up and test the DVD equipment to make sure everything works properly.

Create a worship display in the center of the meeting area. Place items that reflect a water or journey, the candle, basin, pitcher of water, and stones on the cloth-covered table to create the worship center. Make sure there is one stone in the water for each participant. If new members join you for this session, be sure to have some extra smooth river stones available for them to use. Provide an opportunity for newcomers to place their stones in the basin at the end of opening worship. The worship center should be the same in all the sessions.

Place the list of Core Values on a wall or other location in the learning area that is easily visible to all participants. This list of Core Values should remain on display through all the sessions.

Place on a wall or other easily visible location the large sheet of newsprint or poster paper with the sentence: "Vocation is a hands-on activity."

Lead the Session

Gathering and Opening Worship

Greet participants as they arrive. Invite them to make nametags and to find a place to sit.

The Stones and the Water (5 minutes)

Once more, we meet at the basin to begin our session. The prayer time focuses on the important role that wells and water played in the biblical stories and on the importance they still have for much of the world's population. At the well, people meet one another and sometimes meet God.

Welcome participants and invite them to enter a time of prayer. Talk about the importance of water in our lives and how many people in the world live without water security. Because of a scarcity of clean water supplies, many people in impoverished areas must travel many miles to common wells for the water they need. Ask class members to think of something for which we rely on having water (e.g. drinking, bathing, irrigation, etc.). Invite them to share what they have thought of as they close their eyes and begin this time of prayer.

After participants have had time to share their words, slowly pour the water into the bowl from the pitcher. After pouring it in, lift up some water in your hands and let it fall back into the basin.

Have participants slowly open their eyes and pray together this prayer which is found on page 64 of the workbook:

> Jesus, you met a woman at a well
> and asked for something to drink.
> At wells and watering holes, your people gather
> sometimes thirsty,
> sometimes dusty,
> sometimes longing for a splash of something cool.
> We come to this water today
> because our skin is too dry
> and our souls too parched
> for want of your love.
> With all your thirsting children,
> we wait for you here. Amen.

Invite participants to dip their fingers in the water as you light the candle. Those who are new to the group may place their stones into the water at this time.

The Questions

View the Video (8–10 minutes)

Introduce the video segment as follows: "This video segment will help us to claim our vocation as we meet God in the needs of the world."

View the video segment, "Somebody's Calling Your Name."

Ask the following questions:

- What thoughts or questions emerged as you watched "Somebody's Calling Your Name" on the DVD?
- What was your response to Alex's remarks that responding to the needs of the world can be much more than going into a life of service or mission to the poor or disenfranchised in our nation or in others?
- What is your heart's deep gladness? How do you define the world's deep hunger?

Review Journal Work—"Moving Out" (5 minutes)

Ask class members to turn to pages 60–61 in the workbook to the journal exercise "Moving Out."

Invite discussion about how participants responded to this activity. If you engaged in the service/justice activity as a group, talk a bit about what happened. If everyone determined their own activity, allow some time for sharing what they did.

Ask the following questions, based on the journal questions, to help students continue their reflection:

- When did you feel most uncomfortable?
- When did you feel most comfortable?
- What happened during the experience that you want to remember?
- What did you learn about yourself?
- Did you discover any new gifts in the experience? What were they?

Read and Discuss "I Want to Hear My True Name" (8 minutes)

Read the story "I Want to Hear My True Name," pages 64–66 in the workbook.

Invite participants to write responses beneath Devon's and Rabbi Yehuda's quotations as directed in the workbook. Discuss these responses.

Ask the following questions, which are also in the workbook:

- What is different about the true names that Devon and Rabbi Yehuda want to hear?
- What do you think keeps us from hearing our "true" names?

The Scriptures

Do a Responsive Reading of Isaiah 58:1-12

Introduce this segment of the session by asking participants to share what they know about the spiritual practice of fasting.

Read the material about fasting, page 67 in the workbook. Invite participants to talk about what it means to be "hungry for God" as quoted by Lauren Winner, in her book, *Mudhouse Sabbath*, when a rabbi told her, "When you are fasting and you feel hungry, you are to remember that you are really hungry for God."[2]

Introduce the material about Isaiah 58:1-12 in "A Responsive Reading," workbook pages 67–69. Tell the participants that the prophet Isaiah challenged the people of God in his day to see their fasting as more than an individual exercise. Remind students that this passage is written from God's perspective, and ask them to listen for what more God is asking from the people in their fasting.

Form two teams. Team A read the lines marked "A" and Team B read the lines marked "B."

Create a "Faces of Jesus" Collage Based on Matthew 25:31-46

Introduce the biblical reading by saying: "As Jesus told his followers that they would see him in the 'least of these my brothers and sisters' [Matthew 25:40], so we are invited to meet Jesus in marginalized people and places" (NLT). Tell the class that Jesus once told a parable in which persons were judged based on whether or not they had been able to see Jesus in the faces of the poor, the hungry, the thirsty, the ill clothed, the strangers, and the imprisoned. Have someone read the parable in Matthew 25:31-46.

Point out the newspapers and magazines and other materials. Tell the group to look for pictures and events that reflect the needs of our world today and use them to create a collage entitled "Faces of Jesus."

Give the group time to work on their collage together. If your group is very large, you may want to have them create several collages.

Post the collages on the wall and invite comment on the creation and the process:

- Which images or words stand out for you?
- What situations are "calling our names"?
- What feelings did you experience as you worked on this project?

Review "Your Reflections on the Scriptures" (2 minutes)

Tell participants to respond to the question about Isaiah 58:1-12 and Matthew 25:31-46 in the box labeled "Your Reflections on the Scriptures" (workbook, page 71) during the week. They may write or draw their responses. Reassure them that they will not have to talk about their responses unless they want to.

Your Life

This exercise introduces the two concepts to participants and invites them to consider how they are engaged in both acts of compassion and justice. It uses Wesleyan understandings of compassion and justice drawn from the Covenant Discipleship movement.[3]

Define Compassion and Justice (5 minutes)

Invite participants to turn to page 72 in their workbooks. Tell them to consider the two words printed here: *compassion* and *justice*. Ask: "What do you think of when you hear each of these words? What distinguishes them?" Write their responses on a sheet of newsprint that you have posted on the wall or on a white board.

Read the information about compassion and justice, page 72 in the workbook

Invite participants to list examples of each in the space provided in the workbook. Ask them to tell about their examples. List these on another large sheet of newsprint for all to see. Invite reflection around the following questions:

- What are some ways that we can be involved in acts of compassion?
- What are some ways that we can be involved in acts of justice?

Review Core Values List (2 minutes)

Invite participants to look at the list of Core Values in the workbook (page 8) or on the newsprint posted in the learning area. Ask: "Which of these Core Values speak most to you about your name, your vocation, and the needs of the world?" Encourage them to continue this reflection by writing in the Core Values box when they do their journal work each week.

Looking Ahead

Discuss Journal Work—"Getting It Down on Paper"

This is the last week in which class members will have a chance to do journal work in preparation for the session. This exercise asks them to begin sifting through the reflection that they have been doing and to write down learnings and provisional statements of the next steps in their vocational journeys.

Ask participants to turn to pages 74–75 of their workbooks to read the journal exercise for the coming week. Have someone read the assignment out loud. Invite questions about the assignment.

Remind the participants to respond to the questions in the boxes labeled "Your Reflections on the Scriptures" and "Core Values and Your Life."

Closing Worship

Name Calling (5 minutes)

In this worship experience, participants will have the opportunity to hear their name called in blessing and to call the names of others.

Invite participants to recall the importance of true names for Devon and for the rabbi in "I Want to Hear My True Name."

Invite class members to hold hands in a circle. Tell them that they will be asked to offer a brief prayer for the person to their left and to say a blessing for the person to their right. The form of the prayer will be: The group facilitator prays for the person to his or her left, making sure to call the person by name. The prayer should be brief and should include thankfulness for the gifts the person brings to the group.

At the conclusion of the prayer the class member sitting to the left of the person just prayed for should say: *Person's name, God is blessing you and calling your name.*

The prayer continues with the person just blessed offering a prayer for the person to his or her left.

At the conclusion of these prayers, have group members turn to page 75 in the workbook and read the prayer printed there together:

God, who whispers in the night
and shouts in the bright sunshine of creation's glory,
don't let my ears be closed,
don't let my eyes be shut,
don't let my heart be hardened,
don't let my hands be clenched,
but let me be open, ready, willing, and able
to hear my name
and to answer your call. Amen.

---

[1] *Wishful Thinking: A Seeker's ABC,* by Frederick Buechner (HarperSanFrancisco, 1993); page 119.

[2] *Mudhouse Sabbath,* by Lauren F. Winner (Paraclete Press, 2003); pages 90–91.

[3] For more information on the Covenant Discipleship movement, visit the website of The United Methodist Church's General Board of Discipleship at: http://www.gbod.org/smallgroup/cd/. Or see the book, *Guide for Covenant Discipleship Groups,* by Gayle Turner Watson (Discipleship Resources, 2000). Another resource designed for youth and college students is *Together in Love: Covenant Discipleship for Youth,* by David C. Sutherland (Discipleship Resources, 1999).

6

SESSION SIX
TAKING RISKS

Focus:

Risk is an invaluable tool for moving us from who we have been to who we are going to be. By consciously choosing to stretch ourselves into areas where we know we will be required to change, we can stimulate ourselves to greater trust in God and greater awareness of God's call.

Objectives:

- To enable participants to identify a risk they feel they are being called to take
- To create an action plan for their next steps in the vocational journey
- To have class members affirm the gifts of each other as they close this study

Reflections for This Session

Jedediah Purdy, author of *For Common Things*, is a young adult who has thought deeply about the culture of irony that he sees pervading his generation. Purdy talks about the death of idealism in an age where truth can be "spun." Many young people are deeply suspicious of earnestness because they have seen it falter so often and because they believe that values are not so much essential parts of a person's character as they are statements of individuality to be chosen and discarded depending on the image of ourselves we hope to present. Young adults are hesitant to state firm and high-minded convictions because they don't want to look foolish later on. "Recent polls showing that college freshmen have fewer grand hopes and more commitment to making money than ever in memory reveal less the grand avidity of the movie *Wall Street*'s Gordon Gecko than a suspicion that nothing else is quite worth the risk," says Purdy.[1]

Helping young people to value an uncertain future and to stretch into it is a holy task. Jesus' message to his disciples was that the journey they would undertake in his company would be radically contingent and often tenuous. They would look different from the rest of the world around them and they would be looked upon as out-of-touch and even foolish. But there would be a richness and depth to their life, too. They would be a new community formed by Christ's message. And they would begin to reflect God's new order breaking into the world just in the way they were living in it.

In this session, participants will close this study by walking with Ruth and Naomi in a biblical story of risk and by considering what sorts of risk they may be called to take. The character of the next steps in their vocational journey should not be one of ill-considered leaps into the unknown, but of trusting movements in the company of other travelers in which they give their most essential selves to God's new thing. Risk can move us from who we have been to who we shall be.

We will also be drawing this study to a close which provides you the opportunity to help class members consider an action plan for future vocational discernment. You will also want to give students a chance to talk about what they have seen in each other through this study. The final worship act takes us right back to the beginning of this class as we retrieve the stones we placed in the water and carry them with us to a new day.

Prepare for the Session

Let your preparation for the session be a time to pay attention to God and to the needs of group members as well as a time to review the content of the session. Find a quiet and comfortable place where you will not be interrupted. Have the DVD, a Bible, and the workbook available, in addition to the leader guide. Have paper and pen available to jot down notes, insights, and ideas. You may wish to keep these notes in a personal journal during this study.

Pray

Ask for God's guidance as you prepare for the session. Pray for the participants who will be a part of this session.

Read, View, and Reflect

As you read the leader guide, workbook, and Scriptures, and as you view the video segments, write down thoughts, insights, questions, and ideas that emerge for you. Also write questions that you think might emerge from the group.

Review the Core Values described in the introduction (page 10).

Read the Book of Ruth; Numbers 25:1-4; and Deuteronomy 23:3-6. Read background material about the story of Ruth in a Bible commentary such as *The New Interpreter's Bible* (Abingdon Press, 2003). Read "Risky Behavior" on pages 78–79 in the workbook. Think about ways these readings relate to the focus for this session.

View the video segment, "Taking Risks."

Read Session Six, "Taking Risks," in the leader guide and in the workbook. Review the steps in "Lead the Session" in the leader guide.

Pray

Offer gratitude to God for insights, ideas, and guidance for the session. Give thanks for the group members and for what you will experience together.

Gather Materials and Set Up the Learning Area

- Bibles
- DVD, DVD player, and TV
- Leader guide
- Workbooks, have extras on hand for new members
- Nametags and markers or pens
- Chairs in a semicircle for viewing the video
- Small table covered with shiny fabric that suggests water
- Items that reflect water and journey themes, such as a small boat or a spiraling seashell
- A candle, basin, pitcher of water, and some smooth river stones (available at many craft supply stores) for the worship center
- Poster or newsprint with the following sentence: "Live in such a way that your life would not make sense if the gospel were not true."
- A biblical commentary for in-class research

Make sure that your meeting space is a comfortable area for discussion and reflection.

Set up and test the DVD equipment to make sure everything works properly.

Create a worship display in the center of the meeting area. Place items that reflect water or a journey, the candle, basin, pitcher of water, and stones on the cloth-covered table to create the worship center. Make sure there is one stone in the water for each participant. If new members join you for this session, be sure to have some extra smooth river stones available for them to use. Provide an opportunity for newcomers to place their stones in the basin at the end of opening worship. The worship center should be the same in all the sessions.

Place the list of Core Values on a wall or other location in the learning area that is easily visible to all participants. This list of Core Values should remain on display through all the sessions.

Place on a wall or other easily visible location the poster with the sentence, "Live your life in such a way that it would not make sense if the gospel were not true."

Lead the Session

Gathering and Opening Worship

Greet participants as they arrive. Invite them to make nametags and to find a place to sit.

The Stones and the Water (5 minutes)

This opening prayer time draws us once more to the water and prepares us for the closing time when participants will draw out a stone from the water.

Welcome participants. As you gather around the worship area, remind them once again of the significance of the stones and why you placed them in the water. Because you have immersed yourself in this vocational journey together for these weeks, you have been reminding yourselves of God's claim and promise on your lives. Tell them that you will be closing this session by inviting everyone to take a stone from the water.

Ask class members to close their eyes and enter into a time of silence. After an appropriate period of silence, slowly pour the water into the bowl from the pitcher. After pouring it in, lift up some water in your hands and let it fall back into the basin.

Have participants slowly open their eyes and pray together this prayer which is found on page 78 of the workbook:

A voice calls in the wilderness,
"Come, discover your salvation at the margins."
And so we come to live on the edge.
Believing that God is able,
that Christ is sufficient,
that the Spirit is moving across the face of the waters,
we come to live on the edge
of a new and promised day.
Amen.

Invite participants to dip their fingers in the water as you light the candle. Those who are new to the group may place their stones into the water at this time.

The Questions

View the Video (8–10 minutes)

Introduce the video segment as follows: "This video segment will help us to consider the risk of stretching ourselves into areas where we know we will be required to change in order to grow in our trust of God and in our awareness of God's call."

View the video segment, "Taking Risks."

Ask the following questions:

- What thoughts or questions emerged as you watched "Taking Risks" on the DVD?
- How did you respond to the people on the street as they talked about taking risks? With whom did you most identify? Why?
- In the DVD, Alex said, "I would like to reclaim risk as a word that has some positive value." Do you agree or disagree with him? Why?

Discuss "Risky Behavior" (5 minutes)

Introduce the concept of risk as one which has both positive and negative connotations. Some things that seem very risky to some people may feel very natural to others. Ask: "What is something that feels risky to you?" Answers might include everything from jumping out of an airplane with a parachute to speaking in front of a class.

Read "Risky Behavior" on pages 78–79 in the workbook.

Ask the questions below, also on page 79 in the workbook, to stimulate discussion.

- What comes to mind when you hear the phrase "risky behavior"?
- How do you respond to the idea risky behavior is a hallmark of Christian life? In what sense might this be true?
- What risky behaviors might have positive results?

The Scriptures

Read and Discuss Ruth 1:1-18 (10 minutes)

Introduce the biblical reading by explaining that it was a very unusual thing for Israelites to have dealings with Moabites in this day, despite their common ancestry. Stories in Scripture suggest that the people of Moab had led the Israelites astray from serving God, and Israel had responded with hostility toward Moabites. If you have time investigate these passages: Numbers 25:1-4; Deuteronomy 23:3-6. In addition, look at background information about the Book of Ruth in a Bible commentary such as *The New Interpreter's Bible*. One of the things that makes the story of Ruth remarkable is the way it brings together people across mounted prejudices. The end of the story points out that Ruth, a Moabite, was the great-grandmother of Israel's greatest king, David. Ruth also appears as an ancestor of Jesus in Matthew 1:5.

Have one or several volunteers read Ruth 1:1-18. Part of this passage, verses 16-17, is reprinted in the workbook (page 80).

Read the information in the section "Ruth and Risk" on pages 80–81 in the workbook.

Ask the following questions, also on page 81 of the workbook, to help participants gain some clarity about what is happening in this Scripture:

- What is Naomi's most compelling reason for returning home?
  [Responses could include: grief and a desire to return to extended family in Bethlehem, security among her own people, hunger, fear of life in Moab]
- Why does Naomi press Orpah and Ruth to return home?
  [Responses could include: belief that they would be more secure in their home country, belief that God had turned against her, suspicion of Moabites grounded in Israel's stories about them]
- Why might Orpah and Ruth want to go with Naomi?
  [Responses could include: family loyalty, affection, fear of treatment in Moab for having married Israelite men]

- What risks was Ruth taking in making her pledge to Naomi? *[Responses could include: not being accepted in Naomi's home country because she was Moabite, hunger or destitution due to being a widow in a foreign country]*

Review "Your Reflections on the Scriptures" (2 minutes)

Encourage participants to read the entire Book of Ruth during the week and to respond to the questions in the box labeled "Your Reflections on the Scriptures" (workbook, page 82) during the week. They may write or draw their responses. Since this session is the last one, this work will be done on their own.

Your Life

Review Journal Work—"Getting It Down on Paper" (10 minutes)

The journal exercise from the previous week, "Getting It Down on Paper" invited class members to begin formulating visions of where God is leading them. In this segment members will be invited to share some of their reflections growing out of the exercise and to begin to develop an action plan for the next step in the journey.

Tell the class to look at last week's journal exercise on pages 74–75 in the workbook. This exercise asked them to complete some sentences with visions of where God is calling them to be. In particular, the last two questions invited them to think about what they imagine themselves to be in ten years and to articulate the new vision of themselves God has given them through this study. Invite any who wish to do so to share responses to the following open-ended questions from Session Five, pages 74–75 in the workbook:

- To really know me you need to know that I . . .
- The place in my life where God is most at work is . . .
- The needs of the world that are calling my name are . . .
- When I imagine myself ten years from now, I see . . .
- Over the weeks of this study, the new vision God has given me of who I am is . . .

Ask participants to draw a picture using the materials provided or to write about a new vision of themselves as directed on page 83 in the workbook. When they are finished, invite them to tell one another about what they have drawn or written.

Develop an Action Plan (10 minutes)

Ask participants to turn to page 84 of the workbook. Tell them that visions give us a sense of where we feel called to go and they can guide our steps along the way. But the most important question for growth is, What is the *next* step? This page of the student journal asks them to consider where God is calling them to stretch themselves into "risky" territory so that they can hear who they are. Give class members time to complete this exercise. If time allows, ask volunteers to share their action plan.

Review Core Values List (2 minutes)

Invite participants to look at the list of Core Values in the workbook (page 8) or on the newsprint posted in the learning area. Ask, "What do these Core Values say to you about taking risks and trusting God as you pursue a vision of your vocation?" Encourage them to continue referring to their workbooks after this concluding session.

Looking Ahead

Ask participants to read together the quotation written on the newsprint and posted in your room: "Live in such a way that your life would not make sense if the gospel were not true."

Explain that the sentence is adapted from Cardinal Suhard, a former archbishop of Paris, and Steve Long, an associate theology professor at Garrett-Evangelical Theological Seminary, both of whom believe that our actions in the world should be consistent with Christ's teaching and not necessarily in harmony with the world.[2]

Read the paragraph in "Looking Ahead" on page 86 of the workbook. Ask:

- What does this sentence suggest about the relationship of the gospel to the world?
- How risky would it be to live out this sentence in our lives? What would have to change?

Remind the participants to continue to use their workbooks and the journal exercises they have completed even though the group has finished with its meetings. They may wish to return often to the boxes labeled "Your Reflections on the Scriptures" and "Core Values and Your Life" as they continue thinking about their vocation and God's call in their lives.

Closing Worship

Retrieving the Stones

In this closing worship experience, participants will mark the ending of this study by taking a stone from the basin and hearing a word of blessing offered by their fellow class members.

Tell participants to turn to page 86 in the workbook. Read aloud the paragraph in the section "Retrieving the Stones." As directed in the paragraph, participants should write down on that page the name of each of person in the group. Beside each name, they should write one word or short phrase that captures the blessing they have received from this person.

As you begin prayer together, call the name of a member of the class and tell them to retrieve a stone from the water. As they hold their stone, each member of the circle should offer their word or phrase of blessing. Continue until every person has gotten a stone and heard their blessings spoken.

Say the following prayer of thankfulness together, which is printed on page 87 of the workbook:

God of Ruth and Naomi,
you bind together unlikely folks
and bless them in the midst of their uncertainty.
Christ of the table and the cross,
you take the places
where we are blessed and where we curse
and fashion them into instruments of our new identity.
Spirit moving across the waters of creation,
you claim us and call us,
so that we can live on the edge
of what you will do in us today.
Thank you. Amen.

---

[1] *For Common Things: Irony, Trust, and Commitment in America Today,* by Jedediah Purdy (Vintage Books, 2000); page 15.

[2] Emmanuel Cardinal Suhard, Archbishop of Paris, quoted in "Revolutionary of the Heart," by Geoffrey B. Gneuhs, *First Things* (May 1998); available at: http://www.first-things.com/article.php3?id_article=3517. Also adapted from an address given by Steve Long at "Exploration 2000" held in Dallas, TX, Nov. 11–12, 2000.